UNCERTAINTY ADVANTAGE

UNCERTAINTY ADVANTAGE

LEADERSHIP LESSONS FOR TURNING RISK OUTSIDE-IN

GARY S. LYNCH

Copyright © 2017 Gary S. Lynch.

All rights reserved. No part of this book may be used or reproduced by any means, graphic, electronic, or mechanical, including photocopying, recording, taping or by any information storage retrieval system without the written permission of the author except in the case of brief quotations embodied in critical articles and reviews.

This book is a work of non-fiction. Unless otherwise noted, the author and the publisher make no explicit guarantees as to the accuracy of the information contained in this book and in some cases, names of people and places have been altered to protect their privacy.

Archway Publishing books may be ordered through booksellers or by contacting:

Archway Publishing
1663 Liberty Drive
Bloomington, IN 47403
www.archwaypublishing.com
1 (888) 242-5904

Because of the dynamic nature of the Internet, any web addresses or links contained in this book may have changed since publication and may no longer be valid. The views expressed in this work are solely those of the author and do not necessarily reflect the views of the publisher, and the publisher hereby disclaims any responsibility for them.

Any people depicted in stock imagery provided by Thinkstock are models, and such images are being used for illustrative purposes only.
Certain stock imagery © Thinkstock.

Charts courtesy of StockCharts.com.

ISBN: 978-1-4808-3937-3 (sc)
ISBN: 978-1-4808-3939-7 (hc)
ISBN: 978-1-4808-3938-0 (e)

Library of Congress Control Number: 2016920348

Printed in the United States of America.

Archway Publishing rev. date: 6/5/2017

This book is dedicated to man's best friend and mine, Oreo.

Contents

Acknowledgments ix
Prologue xiii

Section I: Turning Risk Outside In: A Market-Driven Strategy to Uncertainty 1
1   The Opportunity 3
2   The Landscape of Uncertainty 29
3   The Transformation Agenda 51

Section II: Principles of Execution 71
4   Focus: The Quest for Market Advantage Should Keep You
    up at Night. 73
5   Navigation: Manage Risk, Navigate Uncertainty 95
6   Urgency: Markets Move Fast, but Organizations Do Not. 113
7   Details: The Devil's in the Details, and This Demands
    Relentless Pursuit 129
8   Priority: Growth Trumps Risk 141

Epilogue: The Circle of Uncertainty 159
Index 169

Acknowledgments

Writing a book is a path to learning about a complex and dynamic topic that is often misunderstood and undervalued. This topic has been the focal point of my career since the 1980s. Beyond the doom and gloom and the next best program for handling an array of threats, my mission has always been the same: Minimize the impact of disruptive events and maximize the risk investment.

Over time, I have seen the importance of reconciling and prioritizing behaviors and the need to neutralize biases. But then something happened as I moved from a role as industry practitioner to a market analyst, management consultant and entrepreneur. Thanks to help from my former boss and now mentor and friend, Craig Goldman, my perspective began to change. Craig introduced me to a community of growth leaders, investors and executives, whose point-of-view about risk went beyond preserving value and operational effectiveness. Their view demanded a more precise understanding of risk and uncertainty that directly tied it to opportunity and competitive strategy.

At the time, risk investments were driven from either a policy, rules, fear, or response point of view. The year Y2k or millennium bug suddenly put risk investments under the performance spotlight. Organizations around the globe had become concerned prior to January 1, 2000 that their computer systems would come crashing down since most of the application code represented the four-digit year with only the final two digits. They also were alarmed to learn that their risk mitigation investment, to fix the code and remediate exposure, would add up to 10-15% of their annual IT budget. For the organization I was working for at the time, the investment represented nearly a half billion

US dollars over three years. Of course, this caught the attention of the Board, investors and executives leading the organization. Risk materially impacted profitability. The era of performance based risk management had begun. Risk had become mainstream but caution prevailed.

Dozens of other risks were introduced or expanded upon such as disruptive technology, geo-political, social class, supply chain and supplier, cyber, and social responsibility. Leaders and managers were suddenly faced with a dilemma that went beyond preserving value and achieving operational excellence. The new challenge was to exploit the opportunity by understanding and leveraging uncertainty as an opportunity and market differentiator or be caught up in risk management and view it as a sunk cost, another necessary but immeasurable program (i.e. return on investment or "check-the-box" exercise). From a personal standpoint, several individuals influence my early thinking over the past decade which inspired me to pursue the "uncertainty advantage". *A special thank you to these key influencers, including Lou Belsito, Gary Mucha, John Michael McConnell, Lenny Goldstein, Bill Topper, Ken Fiorelli, Steve Cobourn, Bob Murphy, Gerry Geisler, Igor Stenmark, and John Merkovsky.*

My goal as an advisor, educator and author is to evangelize the concept that uncertainty and risk are critical elements to competitive strategy and when properly understood and deployed, represent market advantage. My latest research for this book includes twenty four cases and five leadership principles. Many leaders and visionaries were an integral part of the research process. Fortunately, a few people were there for me through the entire process and thus, provided me with the strength and fortitude to finish the project. First, I'd like to acknowledge Michael Thomsett, an experienced author and market analyst. Michael was so much more than a ghostwriter; he was the concrete that allowed the building to be built. For three years, Michael and I went through hundreds of rewrites and a dozen or so changes in direction. Thank you, Michael! I'd also like to thank Karen Avery, senior risk executive, PriceWaterhouseCooper Partner for her support through this process. Karen was a rock whether it was lively debates, questions that help drive the research, challenging the findings or presenting new ideas.

I'd also like to recognize the many executives, leaders and managers who provided input or coordinated to the research. There are a handful who wished not to be mentioned for confidentiality reasons, so I will just offer a simple, "Thank you!" This book would not have been possible without the insight, experience and feedback from a very broad network of leaders and managers. They include: John Krafcik, CEO, Google Self-Driving Car and former CEO Hyundai, North America; Francois Nader, board chairman Acceleron Pharma (XLRN), board director Baxalta (BXLT) and Clementia, former Pdt & CEO NPS Pharma; Dr. Peter Leibinger, vice chairman of the managing board and head of the Laser Technology & Electronics Division, TRUMPF Medizin Systeme GmbH; Doug Hepper, executive chairman Vision-Ease Lens/board of directors/private equity/portfolio company CEO; James Irwin, former product manager Roche and general manager at IMS Healthcare; Rubik Babakanian, SVP & Chief Procurement Officer, Western Digital; Sandor Boyson, executive director, R.H. Smith School, University of Maryland; Jim Rice, deputy director MIT Center for Transportation and Logistics; Brad Phillips, director of strategic sourcing at Rockwell Automation; Grace Woo, supply chain professional, workplace technology strategist; Brian Merkley, global director corporate risk management at Huntsman Corporation; Dan Pengue, former CRO at GE Capital and CFO at EigenRisk Inc.; Michael Burtha, business transformation, knowledge management, change management, and process excellence; John Sokol, vice president technical operations at Otsuka Pharmaceutical Companies (US); and Bindiya Vakil, CEO and founder, Resilinc Corporation.

Finally, I'd like to thank Lois, Josh, Alicia, Michelle, Cruz, and the rest of the crew at the Chester, New Jersey Starbucks. Thank you for the endless stream of caffeine, conversation, community and an environment to hunker down and write for hours at a time!

Prologue

Doubt is the beginning, not the end of wisdom.
George Iles, *Jottings*, 1918

Is it possible that we have been wrong for so many decades? Why do we so often perceive risk as a negative rather than the tremendous opportunity it offers to differentiate between surrender and victory? Why does the business risk narrative so often begin with words such as "contain," "minimize," "reduce," "limit," or "comply"? What if the business narrative was about uncertainty rather than risk, a concept that not only characterizes the unknown with caution but seeks to embrace it as an opportunity? Is a visionary leader differentiated from a risk-averse leader by the way he or she views and pursues uncertainty? For example, the risk-averse leader focuses on only what can be controlled, such as costs and performance, but this misses the essential growth opportunity that invariably accompanies the risk itself.

At the core of this discussion is the dialogue between the historical negative and even defeatist attitude and the more positive and optimistic opportunity that risk presents. By focusing on the benefits that arise from uncertainty, we are able to arrive at a profound realization. Yes, risk often is perceived as a negative. However, it isn't risk that worries us but uncertainty itself. The very idea of "uncertainty" is troubling because no one really knows the outcome, especially if the reaction to it is to circle the wagons and hope for the best. Those leaders who have recognized the opportunities this presents act in a counterintuitive manner and are able to create market advantage. This book demonstrates this as a consistent attribute among leaders who have benefitted from uncertainty. It also provides guidelines for how this strategic out-of-the-box thinking can be institutionalized as part of an organizational strategic plan, a new form of visionary thinking.

How do you as a leader become more visionary by looking at uncertainty differently? Did these words dominate the innovation and growth agenda of great leaders such as Jeff Bezos (Amazon), Elon Musk (PayPal/Tesla/SpaceX), Jack Welch (GE), Howard Schultz (Starbucks), Reed Hastings (Netflix), or Larry Page and Sergey Brin (Google)? I ask because I've come to a few important conclusions based on hard experience, observation, and discussions with heads of industry, government, academia, and other inspirational leaders. These visionary leaders are distinguished from managers by a short list of common attributes and five principles; for example, a market-driven versus compliance- or financial performance–driven mind-set. These are exposed in coming chapters because they demonstrate with clarity the difference between a true innovator, creator, and growth leader and a manager of performance and preservation. It may seem trite to merely observe that "leaders lead while managers only manage," but there is such a powerful aspect to this. That aspect is discovered in the different mind-set, capability, and competencies the true *leader* possesses. Unfortunately, this blend is too often absent in the management of organizations. In those cases where it has emerged, a few individuals have been able to accomplish amazing results. This is the inspiration for this book and for the carefully documented cases it contains. I am certain that I've exposed only a small subset of leaders who have been able to capitalize on the uncertainty mind-set, one they were able to navigate for market advantage. At the very least, bringing forward this point of view among true leaders initiates a discussion and begins our journey.

This can be described by how a leader looks at each "situation", or what they care about most. Is the glass half empty (i.e., a threat or risk to the business) or half full (i.e., a market opportunity)? It is difficult not to look at the world today through the half-empty lens. Disrupters come at us from all directions, threatening desired success and growth. They include technological innovation; new entrants; activism; extreme financial volatility; natural and man-made catastrophes; geo, socio, and political shifts; health epidemics; terrorism; structural change; regulation; and cyber-threats. Combined with increased complexity and a faster rate of change, these disrupters create the worst of all operational environments: unceasing uncertainty. As a result, leaders' efforts to understand and navigate uncertainty often are constrained by competing initiatives, priorities, biases, bad timing, and a perception of the lack of measurable return on investment. Instead, leaders rely on qualitative methods such as gut, instinct, and personal experiences to make critical business decisions. After all, why should they invest the time, attention, resources, and capital or budget to try to understand the uncertainty if it does not lead to greater tangible return? As Albert Einstein once said, "The more I learn, the more I realize how much I don't know." If leaders go forward with the investment in understanding uncertainty, will it open Pandora's box and distract from the business objective? As a leader or manager, do you find yourself getting drawn into a half-empty mind-set? Do regulation, corporate policy, conformance with industry standards, and endless audits/assessments overwhelm your agenda and attention span? Do you find yourself allocating the majority of your discretionary budget to building a moat around the castle rather than expanding your empire? Is risk a burden and uncertainty, something better left to chance or destiny? Or are you like the leaders uncovered in this research for this book? Do you view uncertainty as a half-full scenario that, if navigated efficiently, can result in achieving market advantage? As a manager, are you viewed by leaders as enablers of growth?

About a decade ago, I began to notice a change in the way leaders approached risk and uncertainty. I'm not exactly sure whether by design or out of necessity, but my educated guess would be necessity. At the time, globalization and other factors drove hyper competition, as highlighted in *The World Is Flat: A Brief History of the 21st Century*.[1] To remain

---

[1] Thomas L. Friedman, *The World Is Flat: A Brief History of the 21st Century* (ISBN 1-59397-668-2).

relevant, leaders were forced to make decisions more quickly and, unknowingly in most instances, take on greater risk. Governments and their regulators, media, NGOs (nongovernment organizations), OEMs (original equipment manufacturers), and later social media pushed back on all of this risk taking, especially in the wake of the financial crisis (2008/9), failure of business partners/third parties (2008/12), natural catastrophes in Japan and Thailand (2011), the Deepwater horizon explosion and environmental disaster (2010), sports corruption (2014/5), the collapse of the energy market, and Brexit (2016). "Transparency" became the buzzword of the late 2000s as European Union and US regulators ratcheted up risk and compliance requirements in response after each and every misstep.

It was in 2009 that I noticed a major divergence. Managers became fatigued and apathetic, and as a result, succumbed to what I refer to as the compliance- and rules-based approach to managing risk. However, leaders at organizations such as Starbucks, Roche, Rockwell Automation, TRUMPF, Essilor, NVIDIA, Otsuka Pharmaceutical, and many others pursued a market-driven strategy to navigating uncertainty. After all, the primary business objective did not change; growth leaders needed to take on great uncertainty to not only survive but to thrive in future markets.

This book is about leaders whose half-full point of view is not to ignore but rather embrace, navigate, and leverage uncertainty for market advantage. If this seems counterintuitive, read on. The more than two dozen inspiring cases presented in this book prove the point that beginning with what the market is telling you and then navigating uncertainty is the key to true leadership, whereas, traditional risk management must continue undergoing a great transformation. This book introduces you to leaders who, when faced with great uncertainty, pursued it acutely and understood it in the context of the market and actors (customers, investors, strategic partners, regulators, competitors), developed unique talents, leveraged organizational skills and competencies, sought out innovative capabilities, and then, when the timing was right, pounced on the opportunity to unleash uncertainty as a market differentiator. For these leaders, uncertainty, once seen as a liability, became a precious asset. Market differentiation is not a new concept for these leaders. In fact, it is similar to prior cost, quality, and service-driven structural changes practiced and widely acknowledged. Examples include offshoring, hedging, big box retailing, six sigma, mobile payment systems, and cloud services.

The opportunity to use uncertainty as a market differentiator ignited my passion, bringing greater value to what has traditionally been known as "risk management." The narrative needs to changed because it no longer describes the true underlying activities that it includes. I embrace the opportunity to better understand and define a market-oriented strategy. The irony in all of this is that by putting everything else in my career on hold, I created my own personal uncertainty opportunity.

As this reality became apparent to me, I tapped into a global network of leaders and managers, leveraged more than a decade of application and innovation, and completed three years of extensive research. It became apparent that I needed to put the pen to paper.

The goal: validate the enormous market potential and then extract leadership lessons, principles, competencies, and capabilities so others could use and expand on them.

The hypothesis: growth leaders that navigate uncertainty, rather than just manage risk, will gain measureable market advantage over the next 36-60 months.

I also had to resist the (consultant's) temptation to advocate a new and improved crystal ball for my own purpose. The writing would be the beginning of the journey, not the end. Careful attention to details, nuances, vocabulary, and the speed at which these leaders operated became essentials of the process. The distinctions were subtle but offered tremendous insight to what constitutes a market-driven strategy. For example, "leaders navigate uncertainty, managers manage risk" quickly became one of the foundational principles of this research. The concept of "managing" should be understood as a reactive tactical approach to issues as they arise (versus planning for them in advance). When someone tells you, "We'll manage," it usually means he or she will get by, but just barely. Under prior risk strategies, the idea was to plan ahead for certain well-known risks, as long as the budget was approved for specific activities (buying casualty insurance, taking steps for safety to reduce accidents, monitoring production to reduce errors, diversifying the supply chain). But when it came to the unexpected, no initiatives are taken under this strategy. Rather, when the unexpected occurs, that management philosophy kicks in: "We'll manage." I suggest that when the unexpected (uncertainty) occurs, a new and fresh leadership philosophy should dominate: "We'll innovate."

In 2012, it became abundantly clear from the leaders I interviewed and had worked with that it was the leader who needed to act as the value creator, driver, and owner of the market-driven uncertainty advantage strategy, broadly called the "uncertainty advantage." It was also about that time when it became clear that successful managers in organizations served not only in a risk program management, efficiency, or compliance capacity. Instead, they assumed a value enabler role. They worked hand-in-hand with the leader to address opportunities of a specific business situation. The situation, driven by change, included an opportunity, decisions, assumptions, and a whole lot of uncertainty. The risk capabilities and competencies the manager and others brought to the discussion fit naturally into the business situation and decision. Leaders led and managers managed, as the cliché explains, but with the expanded point of view, this expression took on a profound and deeper significance for me. All of these managers and leaders, I have discovered, are driven by the opportunity for market advantage and are not motivated to manage risk.

Serving as global practice leader for Marsh's Risk Intelligence and Resiliency practice, I leveraged my vast global network of industry, academic, and government leaders while serving in this capacity for an industry giant whose core competence is risk solutions. Although painful at times, living on the road, and circling the globe many time over, the conversations and assignments I experienced provided unprecedented insight. The message was loud and clear; leaders who were crystalizing and then converting their strategies into actions demanded greater insight and access to those with the competencies and capabilities to better understand and leverage uncertainty in support of the business objective. The time came to devote 100 percent of my effort to documenting and bringing these learnings forward. The decision and transition were easy, and the support by senior leadership was overwhelming—despite the fact that the research process went way beyond the original deadline and budget. The response and intrigue about the topic became more evident when I decided to use a LinkedIn feature that allows a member to send a message to someone not in the "connection" list (the InMail feature). I reached out to about a dozen or so CEOs and growth leaders, providing them with a brief summary of the topic, "navigating uncertainty for market advantage." I asked them if they'd be willing to discuss this issue. Intrigued by the subject, all but two responded and set aside time in their busy schedules to discuss the issue. Leading thinkers such as John Krafcik, now Google's CEO of their Self-Driving Car Group, even provided actual cases where their understanding of uncertainty became a market differentiator.

As the research progressed, it became clear that organizations, their leaders, and their managers relied on three dominate mind-sets and strategies for managing risk. They are

- Threat or event driven
- Compliance and/or rules driven
- Performance driven (including asset driven, commonly used by the insurance industry)

Notice something missing? These three mind-sets are designed to preserve value and are internally focused. These strategies are all organization-centric, meaning that risk management has been viewed through the manager's lens outward. This is what I refer to as an "inside-out" strategy. What's missing is the market perspective and the opportunity to create value from uncertainty (remember my previous description of the market actors included customers, investors, strategic partners, competitors, regulators, governments, and interest groups). Didn't business school and practical experience teach us that the priority is the market and all its actors? And didn't we also learn that the business strategy begins with an understanding of the current and future states of the market and market structure, voids and opportunities, competition, and boundaries? How did we forget the market when it came time to managing risk, uncertainty, and compliance? How did we not design for the outside-in perspective? After all, without risk, there is no business opportunity. This was another leadership lesson and principle uncovered in the research: growth trumps risk. Chapter 8 covers this lesson and principle in detail. As an aside, to clarify, I refer to "risk" as the action of choosing the best of the worst possible outcomes. I differentiate this from "uncertainty," which can create either positive or negative outcomes. Now back to the story.

As I began capturing leaders' and managers' behaviors, biases, mind-sets, principles applied, technologies, capabilities, and competencies, I noticed a change in terminology. Instead of "contain," "minimize," "reduce," "limit," or "comply," these leaders used terms such as "opportunity," "differentiation," "innovation," "advantage," "value creation," and "growth driver." For decades, I'd struggled with the "why?" question of risk and uncertainty. I, like so many others, had become experts in the "how" question. Thus, we easily become disconnected from the real value of navigating uncertainty for growth and opportunity.

The book is about purpose, about creating value by understanding and leveraging the uncertainty mind-set. It's a book about the market power of uncertainty above and beyond the weakness of risk management. It's not about elaborate, enterprise-wide programs, endless assessments without action, or simply appointing a "risk guru" or establishing far-reaching hierarchies. It is about reconciling mind-sets, developing and leveraging competencies and capabilities, and unleashing the uncertainty advantage.

Do risk activities create value for the market and leaders? Do they create or accelerate growth opportunities? Do they speed up or improve decision-making? Do they lead to positive discussion and improved performance?

Now, I'm not suggesting that current strategies for managing risk do not have any value. But what I am stating is that their value is limited and should augment a market-driven strategy.

Are you, and you alone, still making decisions based on limited insight into uncertainty? Perhaps your priority is to limit the negative impact of the change, and as a result, you engage in various methods and processes to minimize risk. Growth leaders know what they don't want. But until now, they did not know what they *did* want. As a result, the operational side of the business (not the market-facing leaders) spend most of their time managing large-scale risk programs. They don't have the opportunity to unleash value since they are perpetually trying to preserve the organization's value rather than creating or enhance value.

When I sat down to write this book three years ago, I thought that the primary audience for the book would be leaders, specifically growth leaders. If they were on the hook for driving market value, shouldn't a market-driven strategy have the greatest appeal to them? My thinking evolved as I reflected on so many positive lessons I have learned over the previous seven years. So I researched, I interviewed, I listened. How could I possibly leave out the risk community? This community was my roots, and we risk managers, collectively, were responsible for current strategies, programs, and solutions. Why just the risk community? After all, the operations, finance, technology, and corporate communities also had risk embedded in their everyday responsibilities and decisions. So I decided to lump all of these people into the "manager" category since they typically were not directly responsible for addressing the market. Finally, I had to start at the beginning, the market. If I were going to truly reflect a market-driven strategy, I realized I needed to begin with the market stakeholders—customers, investors, competitors, strategic partners, regulators, governments, and special interest groups. They define the needs and the boundaries, the appetites, tolerances, and thresholds.

Finally, the struggle came to a head. I witnessed the value firsthand and then I saw the light. This book is the beginning of the journey. It documents the inspiration I discovered among the experiences of leaders who successfully understood and leveraged uncertainty as a market differentiator. In this quest for answers, five management behaviors (inhibitors) that prevented value from being extracted from uncertainty rang true. These counterproductive behaviors included risk before growth, financial performance over market opportunity and advantage, speed over insight (or investment in details), checking the box over understanding and exploiting the opportunity, and managing versus navigating.

This is a start, not the final answer, because the trend underway today is dynamic and continuing. The cases I present just begin to scratch the surface. The goal of this book is to initiate and expand the thought process around the benefits of a market-driven strategy and a new way of thinking based not on managing risk but on navigating uncertainty. It's about engaging growth leaders for a particular situation, a change, and discovering how to improve their decision-making processes with a clear vision of not just what to do but why. It's about efficient use of resources, budget, capital, time, and management attention to understand uncertainty and leverage it as a market opportunity. It's also about what Stephen Covey, the famous educator and author, referred to as having the ladder on the right building. You can climb it as fast as you want, but if it's on the wrong building, you are just wasting time, energy, and investment. It's about listening to the market and what it's saying about uncertainty and opportunity, about appetite and tolerance, and about today's versus tomorrow's priorities. Welcome to the journey!

SECTION I

Turning Risk Outside In: A Market-Driven Strategy to Uncertainty

To identify and exploit opportunities, uncertainty is a path to value creation and advantage rather than an exercise in risk. What does this mean? Being willing to consider the interests of those defining your market (customers, investors, competitors, strategic partners, regulators) and pursuing the business opportunity is the path worth taking. This is the essence of market orientation—a view from the outside in—one that quickly identifies, defines, and converts uncertainty into value. Now and then, we all need to slap ourselves to wake up the creative marketing genius and uncertainty navigation skills of the true leader. This section demonstrates how the trifecta of strategy, uncertainty, and transformational thinking overcomes this challenge, showing how leaders can become more opportunistic when facing uncertainty.

The Opportunity

Decisions are about the future and your place in the future when the future is uncertain.[2]

Growth is the holy grail of business and leadership aspiration. Change triggers the growth opportunity, and with it comes great uncertainty. Understanding and navigating this uncertainty environment through a market lens has become the new competitive weapon in the growth leader's arsenal. Differentiators such as cost, service, and quality have long dominated the management mind-set. In a fundamentally uncertain and volatile world, leaders now embrace, deeply understand and are beginning to navigate uncertainty at the speed of business (decision-making). This is a new leadership opportunity and challenge, although it has been viewed traditionally as merely a management challenge. Leaders navigate their way toward growth, whereas managers manage toward performance. A new attribute is what leadership needs and should demand. It is based on a single principle: Don't just manage. Innovate, imagine and relentlessly pursue the uncertainty opportunity for market advantage. This demands application of three essential and

---

[2] Jim Collins, "Foreword," *The Greatest Business Decisions of All Time*, by Verne Harnish (Time Home Entertainment, Inc., 2012).

defining characteristics—uncertainty mind-set, competencies, and capabilities—that serve as the new catalyst to gain market advantage in critical decision-making.

The *Uncertainty Advantage*. What exactly does this even mean?

Just as a starting point, I would like to begin the journey with a company you are of course familiar with: Apple. Whether you subscribe to the outfoxing, blocking or squeezing theory of how Apple keeps the competition at bay with mountains of cash, exceptional equity capitalization, simplicity of product mix, high quality, or simply with broad business intelligence, one fact remains: Apple is the quintessential example of the *Uncertainty Advantage*.

In 2011, Tim Cook revealed that he had entered into long term component supply contracts worth $3.9 billion over the next two years. Apple had locked up 60 percent of the world's touch panel capacity, creating an industry-wide shortage and making it hard, if not impossible, for competition to release new products or keep the shelves filled. Not the first time, or the last, Apple leveraged its deep insight into the market, strategic suppliers and "timing" opportunities throughout its materials-to-customer supply chain to separate themselves from the competition. They exercised similar prowess with batteries, NAND flash memory, LCDs glass for iPad retina display, memory chips, image sensors, and the special resins that are used to hold chipsets together. Events like these delay competitors from coming to market or keeping inventory on the shelves. The key is found in the adage, "You don't have to be the fastest, only faster than your competition." But how can you be that one that stands out, above the crowd, and who spots the real advantage? You can't truly take advantage of uncertainty without a thorough understanding of your market and vision to deliver value to your market. Deep competencies (such as knowledge, diverse talents) and capabilities (such as data and analytics, sensors, visualization) inevitably are called upon at times of change. Apple's competitive strategy and differentiation of activities strategic advantage. A detailed knowledge of sourcing-to-customer activities provided an understanding of inventory levels, pricing, usage patterns, bill-of-material pricing, speed of execution, and customer and supplier capacity. bill-of-material pricing, speed of execution, and customer and supplier capacity. Apple executed quickly and overcame biases by reconciling market, leader and manager mindsets to create a specific market driven focus. This, in a nutshell, is uncertainty, and that is where the visionary is able to identify and exploit it for advantage. Your uncertainty advantage may be closer than you may think! Deep insight, exceptional competencies and advance capabilities likely exist somewhere in your organization. But are they being viewed for good, rather than evil? I say that half-jokingly but the question remains, are your investments in managing risk pointed inward towards preserving organizational value or are they redirected outward, towards the market, where differentiation and opportunity can be translated into creating value? Apple navigated the opportunity afforded by a deep understanding of their market differentiating activities and their willingness to think beyond using the supply chain data to just manage risk.

And that attribute – developing a visionary skill to spot where the advantage is likely to emerge – is what this book is all about. Time again, visionaries like Steve Jobs, Jeff Bezos, Tim Cook, Elon Musk, Andy Grove and others, have spotted their moment and moved boldly to create market advantage when their competitors – often the leaders of organizations – lose their edge just when they need it the most: "A new chief executive officer today, exhausted by the climb to the peak, falls down on the mountaintop and goes to sleep." [3]

Don't make that mistake. With the power of leadership comes great opportunity. Those leaders who seize the moment not only set an example, but discover how to build tomorrow's success from today's uncertainty.

---

[3] Robert Townsend, *Further Up the Organization."* "Leadership." 1984

Imagine a group of folks out for a day of archery. They divide into two teams. The first team, which ended up winning, measured wind speed, made sure their arrows were straight, and understood the angle of fire based on distance to the target. They navigated these obvious uncertainties to improve their accuracy. Not so much for the second team. They spent all of their time improving construction of their quivers, writing up a safety protocol to make sure no one would be injured by a misfired arrow, and strengthening their bows. They overlooked one important aspect, however. They did not have any arrows.

Often in business, and in life, the message and the priorities get confused. Maybe it's because you are performing a "how" or "what" role like the archers on the first team versus those on the second. Or maybe it's because you forgot to ask *why* we should remember to bring arrows. Or we just assumed we knew why, therefore, someone else would remember. Or maybe, you believe that you just don't have to the time to think, just to act. The analogy of business action to the archery range is apt because in it, like in business, we think about aims, targets, competition, and winning.

Throughout my career, I found this was too often the case when addressing the topics of risk and uncertainty. The result has been lost opportunity, slow growth due to unjustified cost and self-imposed delays, distractions caused by checklists and endless functional assessments, and many frustrated business executives. More about this in a moment.

In November 2011, I was invited to join a new group established by the US Department of Commerce called the Advisory Committee on Supply Chain Competitiveness.[4] Belonging to this committee was an eye-opener and led in part to the creation of this book. I thought if we as a nation are looking to become more competitive, why not begin by looking at uncertainty and the way risk is managed? Sure, we can compete on cost, service, and quality. But what about understanding

---

[4] In accordance with 15 U.S.C. 1512 and the Federal Advisory Committee Act (FACA), as amended, 5 U.S.C., App., and with the concurrence of the General Services Administration.

and navigating uncertainty to gain market advantage over competing global economies. How could this collective group, with it's vast understanding of uncertainty, enable organizations to move faster and take on more risk?

The committee's mission was to improve the nation's trade performance and competitiveness by assessing regulatory policies affecting US supply chains.[5] My mission in serving on the committee was to introduce the concept of understanding and navigating uncertainty and its importance in creating market advantage (based on the idea that from risk comes opportunity). Several years earlier, I was involved in a different mission with similar goals for the World Economic Forum's Global Risk Network (*Building Resilience in Supply Chains*[6]). This experience uncovered market opportunities and rewarded organizations for their investments in understanding and managing supply chain risk and uncertainty. As an example, risk financing and transfer products were created. As witnessed by these two initiatives and the two dozen plus cases in this book, the uncertainty advantage can be applied at an industry or macro level as well as at the organization or micro level.

In other words, it all begins with an understanding of uncertainty or should I say, a willingness to take the time to understand uncertainty in the same way that we understand cost structures and our customers. Understanding uncertainty is not limited to measuring risk or selecting the best of the worst possible outcomes. This is a profound change of course from the past, where reactive risk management systems dominated the thinking of leaders (including myself). Over many years, I have begun to realize the tremendous opportunities in navigating uncertainty and limitations of past risk strategies as a better path to trying to manage risk. I have completely and profoundly rethought all of my old assumptions on the subject. This is where and why I began to think in a different way: *Don't manage. Innovate, imagine and relentlessly*

---

[5] http://trade.gov/td/services/oscpb/supplychain/acscc/about.html.
[6] http://www3.weforum.org/docs/WEF_RRN_MO_BuildingResilienceSupply Chains_Report_2013.pdf.

pursue the uncertainty opportunity for market advantage. View uncertainty as an opportunity and risk as exposure.

Thus began my journey into the realm of uncertainty.

A market-driven strategy to navigating uncertainty is designed to create rather than just preserve value. To be clear, I'm not suggesting abandoning currently deployed value preservation risk management strategies. Let me repeat that, prior strategies for managing risk have value although defensive and the competencies and capabilities of the individuals and organizations are what enables a market driven strategy. What I am suggesting is to consider exploring and augmenting your current (enterprise) risk strategies with a market-driven strategy designed specifically to create value and growth by leveraging uncertainty rather than by avoiding it. For example, the Hyundai North America leaders gained market advantage during a time when few people wanted to purchase an automobile because of severe economic uncertainty. Leadership did not devote their entire attention to managing the operational implications of the demand downturn (such as reducing inventory) but instead sought out deep intelligence about structural design of the auto industry's vulnerabilities and its relationship to market behaviors. They augmented the performance based risk strategy with competencies and capabilities to understand how change could create a differentiator then and exploiting uncertainty by leveraging lessons learned in Germany. They were able to get to the market three weeks sooner than their competitors and sell out their inventory. More about Hyundai's success later in this chapter. Could the same be true of a change like BREXIT, (i.e. when Great Britain decided to exit the European Union)? The preservation only strategy would recoil and take defensive action to address the implications of BREXIT such as an estimated 15% devaluation of the pound, the potential loss of talent as European nationals returned home and risk presented to pharmaceutical exports.[7] But who was thinking about the opportunity? What organizations embraced the mindset that this change could be an opportunity and possessed the competencies and capabilities to capitalize on uncertainty? As described in the Financial Times article, *Brexit — an opportunity as well as a threat*", Peter Brooks, Head of Behavioural Finance, Wealth and Investment Management, Barclays stated, "Market turmoil can turn out to be a source of value for investors. This is not to say that markets are not still risky — they are — but in times of stress, markets are not only pricing in rational risk expectations, but they also price in the emotional anxiety of all those investors who have taken their eyes off their long-term goals. So, unless we think that markets are significantly underestimating the true risks, then times of turmoil are good entry points for long-term investors."[8]

As the question goes, ask a manager why there are brakes on automobiles, and the answer will be "To stop or slow down." Ask a growth leader the same question, and the answer will be, "Brakes allow us to go faster." It's a different mind-set.

In an interview with John Krafcik, former CEO of Hyundai North America and now chief executive officer for Self-Driving Car Project, Alphabet Inc. summed up the current state and this mindset as,

> "It's not something I've seen consistently and I've often wondered why more companies are not more opportunistic; why isn't this a natural strand of DNA. It doesn't seem to be."

An Underdog Automotive Company Unleashes the Uncertainty Advantage

An example of how an organization created market advantage is the case of Hyundai Motors. In 2008 and 2009, the recession in the United States deeply affected auto sales. As John Krafcik, CEO of Hyundai

---

[7] *Out and down: Mapping the impact of Brexit*, Economist Intelligence Unit, 2016.
[8] Peter Brooks, *Brexit – an opportunity as well as a threat*, Financial Times, July 6, 2016.

Motors American (HMA) explained in an interview for this book, "It was time of chaos. But we had the right leadership team on the ground in the U.S. We were able to take advantage of uncertainty." They also had laser-like focus and decided to initiate change and leadership tapped into management's deep knowledge of uncertainty. The "situation" was clear and the question well understood. How do we leverage enormous market uncertainty into a positive buying force? The markers indicated that this would be a material and speculative change and that the time was right to pursue uncertainty as a positive force and as a market differentiator.

The "right" leadership team has to consist, at the very least, of a strong growth leader able to act decisively on good information/intelligence and in recognition of market advantage to be gained; strong support from the team itself without resistance to the introduction of new ideas, and, of course, a value enabler who can bring good ideas to the decision maker. So rather than looking at the recession as a problem, Krafcik said that recession, "enabled us to lean into market anxiety."

Even beyond this, the growth leader and team needed a requisite mind-set, an awareness of the uncertainty advantage and how to recognize it. They needed to understand how their competitors and other stakeholders interpreted the same facts to reach different conclusions. The growth leader and his team had to imagine how, during a recession affecting auto sales, the opportunity presented itself when the buying public was unsure of its own future. Yes, this was a problem; but it was also an opportunity. What could Krafcik's team do to improve the belief in their hypothesis that the market wanted to buy new cars but were too afraid to enter into a loan agreement that offered no way out? The overcapacity and over-leveraging in the used car market was a reality that most buyers had been exposed to via the earlier home-lending crisis. How could this fear be turned into confidence? That was the challenge of the moment.

People were not buying cars, and the reason was well understood by Hyundai. "Dramatic drop-off in car sales was due a general sense in the public that people were losing their jobs everywhere. We recognized that people weren't buying cars out of fear of losing their jobs," Krafcik explained. Hyundai discovered that it was possible to navigate this situation to create market advantage. The key was to identify what would convince the buying public that, in spite of the economic trouble of the times, there were sound reasons to buy new cars. They used a creative system, allowing buyers to return their cars if they lost their jobs later. How was this accomplished? Creatively! Being the smaller player had its distinct advantage. The smaller player typically has greater urgency and much more open field to navigate.

At that time, an insurance company (EFG) had gone to the Big Three auto manufacturers with an idea to solve this problem, but all three companies rejected it. The timing was right once the company came to Hyundai. Their idea led to development of the Hyundai Assurance Program. Customers were able to take their new cars back to the dealer and give them up if they lost their job, and there was no negative effects on their credit scores. Krafcik touched on the core issue: "We saw this as an opportunity."

Why did Hyundai recognize the value of this program when the other auto companies had not? The differentiator was that Hyundai's management team had a growth leader, market-driven mind-set, and performed its internal analysis to better understand uncertainty among customers and competitors. Hyundai had greater confidence than their competitors, which translated into market advantage. Hyundai performed a deep analysis of customer demand, supplier capabilities and competitor positioning as part of their strategic analysis. They understood that their competitors might be complacent, confused, or that their bureaucratic structures would not support quick action. In their quest for improving operational effectiveness, operations and financial management only considered supply side risk; in other words, risk exposure of the organization and the priority of value preservation. The growth leader tackles demand side risk, meaning developing an appreciation of market concerns: the customer, investor, regulator, and partner. Why were car sales falling, and what could Hyundai do to change this?

Once Hyundai made arrangements with the insurer, things moved fast. In thirty-seven days of their first meeting, Hyundai had an ad running during the NFL championship game. Krafcik said, "It rocked the world." In other words, by displaying confidence to the buying public, Hyundai demonstrated that it understood the demand issues, even in uncertain times.

The great lesson is clear; companies that commit to deeply understanding the origins of uncertainty and reconcile mind-sets (market, leaders, and managers) can better address it. Listen for it, sense it, pounce on it when it arises. The individual that typically focuses on operational excellence, the value enabler, acts as an intermediary and provides the capabilities and competencies in such cases, taking solutions to support change and the growth leader's decisions. That growth leader is then able to improve critical decision-making. This can all take place, based on the Hyundai example, in about thirty-seven days. But it required participation from the value enabler within the organization.

> **Value Enabler:** The individual(s) within the organization, usually a manager, with the ability to recognize the crucial steps required to put a program into effect and who is able and willing to support the growth leader and the decisions that leader needs to make.

That value enabler can come from anywhere inside or outside of the organization. So as much as any other attributes, a growth leader should seek value enablers and be prepared to take action. The value enablers should adopt the market-driven mind-set as well, embracing a great sense of urgency in providing the capabilities and competencies for the "situation" and business decisions. The solution in Hyundai's case was focused not on operational or financial risks but on what helped the key stakeholders (in this case, customers). It also enhanced prospects for other stakeholders, including investors and regulators. Rather than relying on government bailouts like the Big Three did during this time, Hyundai arrived at an effective market solution aimed at helping customers feel safe about buying cars.

Who's Point of View?

I'd like to begin the journey into the uncertainty advantage by introducing three actors: the market, the leader, and the manager. The **market** represents the *why,* much like the team on the archery range. The market consists of customers, investors, strategic partners, regulators, competitors, governments, and special interest groups. The market actor will always be our first order of business or action.

The **leader**, on the other hand, represents the *what* and *when,* or the archery team member calculating wind direction and angle of shot based on distance. The leader in the organization, better described as the growth leader, drives sustainable growth and value into the market. Growth leaders come in all shapes and sizes. They can be a CEO, group general manager, hedge fund manager, underwriter, profit-and-loss leader, product/product category executive, innovator, or brand owner. The point is that the growth leader defines *what* needs to be done and *when* it should be done in order to meet the *why* of the market. Their actions include the value proposition, innovation, partnership, investment, better service, higher quality, greater commitment to the community, raising capital, instilling confidence, and now, thoroughly understanding and navigating uncertainty for market advantage.

The **manager** represents the *how,* or the archer who starts out by understanding wind direction and distance to the target. The manager may have direct or indirect responsibility for risk and uncertainty. Direct responsibility includes those whose full-time functional role includes risk management. Examples include risk program managers such as risk and insurance, environmental, health, safety, quality, security, cybersecurity, legal, and compliance. They typically are aligned with and assigned support for a dedicated risk program. Indirect responsibility includes those whose full-time role included risk and uncertainty activities (by the way, that should be everyone).

Examples include operations, technology, or finance managers whose primary day-to-day responsibility is to optimize performance and deliver value.

> Have you ever confused the roles and priorities?
> Have you tapped the uncertainty advantage?

> **Growth Leader:** Market-facing, responsible for driving growth and value, and empowered to make key decisions to initiate and sustain growth.
>
> **Manager:** The individual responsible for performance-driven decisions, coordinating resources for the purpose of optimizing and preserving value. The manager may have direct or indirect responsibility for risk. An example of direct or dedicated responsibility include risk/insurance managers such as environmental, health, safety, security, quality, third party. Managers with indirect responsibilities include those in operations, technology, finance, legal, communications, and human resources.
>
> **Markets:** The demand side of the business that defines and measures value,[9] including investors, customers, competitors, regulators, strategic partners, governments, communities, and special interest groups.

"Leaders prepare the organization for change," as described by John P. Kotter in his timeless 2001 *Harvard Business Review* article titled "What Leaders Do." By contrast, armies of managers adopt a preservation mind-set as they cope with complexity, performance, consistency, and

---

[9] "Markets" encompasses the concept of "competitive well-being" of a business as defined by Michael Porter, "The Five Competitive Forces that Shape Strategy," *Harvard Business Review,* January 2008), pp. 86–104.

quality issues within their own functions or organizational boundaries. This culture, mind-set, and associated strategy leads to fiefdoms, excessive cost from inefficiencies and redundancy, as well as accountability gray areas or gaps. It also creates a truly destructive management style, which, bluntly put, can only be called decision paralysis, a selfishness or "me-ness" mentality and dysfunctional functional operations (similar to that of a dysfunctional family[10]). As a result, there is lack of engagement between the growth leader and those managers with the responsibility for actively and directly managing risk. The former wants to innovate, but the latter wants only to manage. The by-product is an organization littered with stand-alone risk programs, unsubstantiated methods for measuring risk, self-serving analytics and performance metrics, poorly defined budgets for equally undefined programs, and what one leading management consultant refers to as perhaps the organizations greatest risk—the risk program and false confidence it provides.[11] The problem is further exacerbated by organizational structures where lower-level managers report to middle managers, and these managers report to higher levels of management. A middle management disconnect or misstep has a viral effect on lower-level management, especially when middle management fails to address risk challenges in the same way they address performance challenges. If the middle manager communicates a compliance based or "check the box" risk strategy than expect an army of lower level management deploying checklists, assessments and surveys. All management may have assignments to perform, but like an archery team, did anyone remember to bring the arrows? In the hierarchy of management, the prevailing view is value preservation and balancing risk with performance, compliance, or impending threats. Biases, functional orientation and incentives, inadequate or limited capabilities or competencies, lack of focus, and a belief that appointing a "risk czar" or programs that boil the ocean (i.e., broad-based enterprise

---

[10] David Stoop and James Masteller (1997-02-10). *Forgiving Our Parents, Forgiving Ourselves: Healing Adult Children of Dysfunctional Families*. Regal. ISBN 978-0830734238.
[11] Doug Hubbard, "The Failure of Risk Management: Why It's Broken and How to Fix It" (Wiley, April 2009).

programs that lack engagement, incentive, and relevancy) dominate. There is paralysis.

The concept of "Don't manage. Innovate, imagine and relentlessly pursue the uncertainty opportunity for market advantage." presents a solution to this deep and pervasive disconnect amongst the market, leaders and managers. However, by taking a fresh look at the nature of uncertainty, we can reconcile the differences. Fortunately, the transformation has begun, led by the growth leaders, those archers who understand the importance of bringing arrows to the range. They have taken the initiative on their own, uncovered opportunities, improved their competence and awareness of opportunities, increased their capabilities, and acknowledged the urgency and time sensitivity to identify and respond to uncertainty opportunities. Both sides bring value to the table, but in different ways. Management is an essential skill for running the operation. Managers are the cooks who keep pots from boiling over or baked goods from burning. Leaders are responsible for writing new recipes and bringing them to the kitchen. Working together, leaders and managers discover that both sides have worthwhile skills. With an inside out strategy, the tendency is to take sides, with one side having to be right and the other having to be wrong. With an outside in strategy, everyone has an essential role to play. The two sides reconcile their differences by better understanding their roles.

Bottom line, the market-driven strategy demands *leaders first*, followed by *managers*, to navigate the market-driven strategy and understand uncertainty as an integral part of critical decision-making. Organizations need both, but progress relies on growth leadership. Leaders already have their foot on the gas. To gain the uncertainty advantage the organization must reconcile the market, leader and manager mindset. Specifically the market and leader, leader and manager and manager to market mindsets must be in sync. The uncertainty advantage mind-set relies on the confidence and intelligence to move faster into the unknown. To do this, the leader relies on deeper competencies and broader capabilities to uncover market opportunity.

By reconciling the mind-sets of market, leaders, and managers, you will be able to take an enormous step in the transformation toward market advantage. Opportunities that uncover market advantage, coordinated among these actors, create dramatic results and effective navigational outcomes. However, they seldom align or take into account one another's point of view.

Illustration 1: Reconciling Uncertainty Mindsets

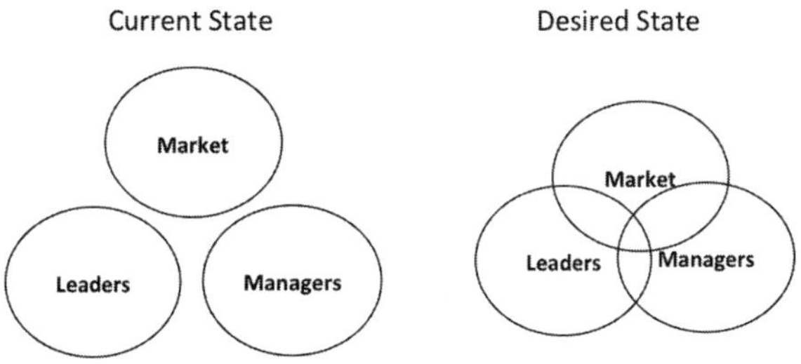

Current State

- Market
- Leaders
- Managers

Desired State

- Market
- Leaders
- Managers

Illustration 2: Universe of Actors

Market
- Customers
- Competitors
- Investors
- Regulators
- Strategic Partners
- Governments
- Special Interests

Actors

Managers
- Marketing
- Sales
- Operations
- Finance
- Technology
- Risk, Audit & Compliance
- Program
  - Quality, Security, Environmental, Health, Safety

Leaders
- CEO
- Competitors
- Directors
- Regulators
- Profit/Loss Leaders
- Underwriters
- Special Interests

Market Driven and the Situation: A New Paradigm

Where do we begin? With the previously described growth leader leading the change and a "situation", brought about by change. A growth leader, as we've defined, drives market value and growth (versus a manager who is responsible for optimizing operational and financial performance). The "**situation**" includes a specific change, opportunity, assumptions, decisions, and uncertainty. It's what the leader cares about most. It's important to note that I am not referring to all change. A market-driven strategy requires time, attention, budget, and resources and, therefore, is best applied to structural, material, and disruptive types of change.

Illustration 3: The **Situation**

> Change can be triggered by physical events such as natural catastrophes like earthquakes, hurricanes, typhoons, and floods or health epidemics and pandemics; or man-made events like fires, sabotage, or human errors. Other changes are nonphysical. These include structural changes in the market (foreign exchange, credit, commodity, activism) and disruptive innovation, shift in pricing parity, shrinkage or expansion in capital markets, organizational transformation, regulation, new entrants, and shift to the core business strategy).

Let's look more closely at a case study that dramatically makes the point about a market-driven situation. It began when a pharmaceutical company and its growth leaders detected the possibility of unprecedented structural change at many levels—economic, social, health, jurisdictional, and geopolitical change. The change or triggering event was the spread of a highly pathogenic virus. They, as well as the broader universe of the market, leaders, and managers had prior experience with a similar virus but on a smaller scale when, in 2002, an outbreak of SARS (severe acute respiratory syndrome) had occurred in Asia Pacific. The virus spread quickly, infecting people in more than thirty-seven countries within a six-month period (November 2002 through July 2003). The event paralyzed Hong Kong's and China's agriculture, hospitality, and transportation industries. It impacted industries in Singapore and Ontario, Canada. Fast-forward now. It's four years later, and global business is being led by vast interconnectivity and interoperability of supply chains, foreign direct investment, and an enormous uptick in domestic and international travel. A new virus, avian flu virus (or H5N1) appeared on the scene. Sparked by the change to global business, the loss estimates from a similar epidemic or pandemic skyrocketed to more than 4.8 percent of global GDP, or more than $3 trillion in estimated losses.[12] Experts modeled the velocity of the spread at potentially as high as 35 percent of the world population within thirty days.[13] Change brought about by an imposing event, such as the 2005/2006 H5N1/avian flu and similar viruses in 2009 (H1N1/swine flu) and 2014 (Ebola outbreak), created both exposure and opportunity.

One organization and its growth leaders that I had the pleasure of working with decided to do both—manage the exposure while embracing, understanding, navigating, and leveraging uncertainty for market advantage. Armed with the uncertainty advantage mind-set,

---

[12] http://www.worldbank.org/content/dam/Worldbank/document/HDN/Health/WDR14_bp_Pandemic_Risk_Jonas.pdf, page 2.
[13] Center for Disease Control and Prevention, www.cdc.gov.

the growth leader quickly surmised that change triggered a growth opportunity.

Case Study: Roche and the Market-Driven Strategy to Navigating Uncertainty

The Situation: possibility of unprecedented structural change at many levels—economic, social, health, jurisdictional, and geopolitical change. The change or triggering event was the spread of a highly pathogenic virus creating an opportunity for the broader distribution of an already successful anti-viral product.

The (potential) Change: Highly pathogenic virus that threatened the global workforce and flow of materials, products, services, information, and cash.

The Opportunity: Commercialize Tamiflu®, an effective anti-viral that had previously targeted the government and public health market. Roche's economic opportunity potential estimated at $1billion+ in new revenue for the commercial market and social responsibility.

Expected Outcomes and Critical Business Decisions: How much to invest in manufacturing capability, inventory; how fast to invest; how to market to the commercial (a new) customer; how to overcome regulatory challenges at a global, regional, and state levels; how to move product in a constrained network; how to distribute and manage inventory; how to prescribe or distribute; how to address security and safety concerns over the whole operation; how to educate the buying audience; and how to prioritize and segment industry, markets, and buyers.

Uncertainty: Massive potential economic, social, health, jurisdictional, and geopolitical implications. For Roche, a significant investment in manufacturing and distribution capability for an event with unknown likelihood and outcomes.

Strategy: Market based to navigate uncertainty for economic, social and brand advantage and an event based strategy for preserving Roche's value and ability to operate.

For the manager, the possibility of a global pandemic represented unprecedented and unimaginable structural change. The economic, social, health, and jurisdiction consequences of a market shift of this magnitude could lead to a shortage of materials and skills, lack of mobility, inability to produce due to a shutdown in infrastructure services (energy, utilities, communications, sanitation, transportation), or a chaotic and risky distribution network threatened by social disorder. Maintaining current performance levels would be impossible. The only alternative perceived by management was to hunker down, prioritize risk prevention and mitigation activities, and ride out the storm. For the leader whose mind-set, capabilities, and/or competencies were in demand by the market, the situation represented a growth opportunity, precise decisions, well-researched assumptions, and thorough understanding of uncertainty. One company, F. Hoffmann-La Roche Pharmaceuticals, led by James Irwin, Tamiflu product leader, recognized the opportunity as well as the uncertainty advantage. James knew that he could leverage the organization's extensive knowledge of the viruses, societal lessons from the SARS experience, marketing savvy, logistics and distribution expertise, and antiviral product, Tamiflu®. But first, they needed to deeply understand uncertainty and all it had to offer.

At the time, Tamiflu® was one of only two antiviral drugs that minimized the spread of a high mortality and fast-moving disease, the H5N1; no vaccine existed. This led to an opportunity arising from the change, and in this instance, also a potential crisis for many. As the growth leader, James pursued a more thorough understanding of uncertainty and by doing so, improved his degree of belief in his market assumptions for sales, sourcing, production, and distribution. Key to his success was his willingness to engage the market, other leaders, and managers, and reconcile their mind-sets. His goal at the onset was to coordinate their motivations, incentives, biases, and beliefs.

What were some of the critical decisions James needed to make, and what was the uncertainty he needed to know more about to convert and leverage in the form of market advantage?

- *Investment priorities and timing,* such as when will the virus materialize, how fast will the events unfold, how big is the opportunity and over what period of time, what are the competitor's capabilities, competencies and mindset, and what industries and geographies have the most to lose?
- *Operations and logistics activities,* such as where would the drug be produced and warehoused, how would it be distributed, how much to manufacture and when (what's the schedule), and how will the drugs be dispensed (logistics as well as the approved process for distributing a prescription drug)?
- *Regulatory challenges,* such as what were the regulatory obstacles by country?
- *Pricing questions,* such as will organizations pre-purchase or contract for the drug and at what price?

Here is what James faced. The first challenge was for the leader to define and promote a market-driven mind-set to uncover the actual opportunity. At the time, the drug was sold retail and primarily distributed for pandemic use to public sector health organizations such as the World Health Organization (WHO) and German, French, and US health organizations (Atlanta-based Centers for Disease Control and Prevention). Irwin looked beyond the urgent health concern to the organization (which another part of the organization was addressing) and identified the opportunity available in distributing directly to the private sector, which was potentially estimated to be a $1 billion opportunity. This required the growth leader to adopt a market-driven mind-set, involving navigation of a complex set of decisions. Why? Because with only government distribution, commercial organizations could not guarantee immediate access to the drug without an expanded market. Irwin summed it up the best: "To make supply chain happen you have to have your people driving trucks, doing the finance, sourcing the goods. You can have all the plans in the world but if you don't have your people, supply chains won't function. It's as simple as that."[14]

By relentlessly pursuing the market-driven nature of uncertainty, Roche was able to expedite decisions and empower their broad marketing and distribution network. They were able to quickly convert uncertainty into opportunity. But this was no simple task. It involved investment of capital to fund production (investor), distribution, and storage (logistics); managing public perception (patients, doctors, regulators) and dealing with how to approach a different buying audience (patients, doctors, wholesalers); obtaining product liability coverage (finance, treasury, risk management); and the range of complexity involved with forecasting, scheduling, global logistics, inventory management (sourcing, operations, IT, and logistics); and multi-regulatory agency scrutiny (regulators). The risk was extreme, but the opportunity, if approached with the right mind-set, competency, and capabilities, represented the potential for a multibillion dollar market advantage.

Show Me the Value

What value can be gained from a market-centric strategy and a growth leader who embraces, understands, and leverages uncertainty as a differentiator?

The process of interviewing uncovered many insights, leading to better definition of "value" for organizations. You don't measure success just by creating new products in the market. You have choices: (1) you can go on offense (leveraging competencies and capabilities to create opportunity); (2) you can go on defense to avoid and navigate around bad things, negative events and changes, and even black swans; (3) you

---

[14] Gary S. Lynch, "Single Point of Failure: The 10 Essential Laws of Supply Chain Risk Management", Wiley, 2009.

can make better, more-informed decisions consistently closer to the bull's-eye than all your competitors, which gets a better yield because you tapped into understanding uncertainty at a level others have not; or (4) you can improve margins by focusing on limited investments and the situations that matter most (and will have the greatest upside or downside impact). Here is a summary of gains as described by the leaders I have spoken and worked with over the past decade.

- Create new revenue and growth opportunities (market growth; leveraging competencies and capabilities as previously described in the Roche example); leadership lessons from Hyundai, Starbucks, Intel, Roche, Marsh, AIG/Lexington, Zurich, McCormick and Company, and General Motors.
- Establish market advantage via better, faster, and more accurate decision-making (i.e., more precise anticipation and response to the market precision and agility; greater customer, investor, and regulator confidence and trust; uncover investment opportunities that yield significant returns on behalf of the client or market); leadership lessons from TRUMPF, Huntsman, Whirlpool, Volkswagen, and retail and textile industries.
- Improve performance via greater efficiency and return in the allocation of risk resources (market efficiency; derived from a more efficient and effective allocation of time, management attention, resources, and capital or budget); measurable improvement in risk reduction (market confidence and greater relevance, including better "risconomics"1, i.e. allocating precious risk resources to that which is most important to the business); leadership lessons from Rockwell Automation, NVIDIA, Western Digital, Otsuka Pharmaceutical, Nokia, NPS Pharma, TJMax, Chrysler, and the automotive industry.

To summarize, the uncertainty advantage as a measure represents how quickly, efficiently, and comprehensively an organization understands, assimilates, makes relevant, and executes (or reacts to) the unknown as part of critical decision-making. It should be adopted as a key component of business decision-making and growth strategy.

A final observation but one of critical importance.

> Markets move fast, but organizations do not.

This is a critical point; one I return to throughout the book. Market advantage is short-lived and must be acted on quickly. I do not suggest a gut reaction to discovered uncertainty. Essential to this process is a calm and analytical study of the issue, not rushed but efficiently considered. This does not mean endless committee meetings and reports, but it does mean bringing together all of the essential resources. It also means considering alternatives before determining how to proceed. This process has to be thorough and accomplished completely, but it has to take priority. Only when the problem and solution have been defined and agreed upon is it time for action., But once there, action has to be fast and immediate because market advantage will disappear as quickly as it appears.

Together, the calendar (discussed in chapter 7) and the clock reflect urgency and the best timing for exploiting the opportunity. How fast should you go, and what are the new paths to pursue? Is there an optimal time of the year for execution, one whereby the markets are stronger or competitors weaker? Do you truly understand the opportunity that uncertainty may play in accelerating or hindering the journey? Going fast in business demands that uncertainty navigation responds quickly.

As part of the market transformation, growth leaders advance by understanding and defining boundaries or acceptable levels of market uncertainty, appetite (how far and fast to go), and tolerance (the degree of pain one is willing to accept for a given return). Contrary to the widely held belief that executives define an organization's risk appetite and tolerance, the market-driven strategy begins when the market establishes the boundaries. True market advantage is the key to creating growth. In risk management, the mind-set is different; it is focused on value preservation.

Market advantage is achieved by satisfying the needs of one, some, or all of these stakeholders. Industry, geography, and other market segmentation predefines the boundaries in many respects. For example, Facebook CEO, Mark Zuckerberg's stated that "in a world that is changing really quickly, the only strategy that is guaranteed to fail is not taking risks."[15] The market of Facebook customers, investors, regulators, and competitors defines the degree of risk that is permissible. However, as Francois Nader (board chairman, Acceleron Pharma and former CEO, NPS Pharma) pointed out in an interview, "as a director or executive of a pharmaceutical company, conceptually what he is saying makes sense; however, in my business it could be disastrous if the risk I take, jeopardizes the health and safety of the patients." The point here is that the market ultimately presents the opportunity and defines the boundaries. Market advantage is where the uncertainty advantage mind-set begins.

The key point to remember is this. The uncertainty advantage is a strategy for creating value and driving growth. Uncertainty introduces the unknown, but in most instances, it also introduces an opportunity. How you versus the market understand, anticipate, respond, and execute during uncertain times can determine whether you wind up as Netflix or Blockbuster.

Uncertainty is most prevalent when major change occurs, whether self-initiated or imposed by external forces (such as acquisition, natural disaster, or investor activism). Risk management, on the other hand, represents a process, structure, rules, and methods to identify and measure the best of the worst outcomes for reducing risk. Risk mitigation strategies are about preserving value when reacting and responding to ambiguity, doubt, volatility, and the unknown. These strategies are

---

[15] http://www.brainyquote.com/quotes/quotes/m/markzucker453450.html.

often compromised of programs, assessments and audits, and rules and compliance requirements.

Growth versus risk is the eternal and predisposed conflict between leaders driving growth strategy and managers whose full-time responsibility it is to optimize performance and improve efficiency and margins while managing an endless universe of risk (compliance, security, health, safety, and audit management). Where do you stand? Are you operating at the intersection of business strategy and risk or in the crosshairs of growth and performance? Are you adding value to the strategic decision-making process, or are these decisions—the ones that contain massive potential risk and uncertainty—delegated to others, only to be deferred until later in the life cycle? What is your level of insight into uncertainty, and are you leveraging to gain market advantage?

What if those whose responsibility it is to manage risk were able to transform a value preservation mind-set into one of value creation and enablement. Of course, this can only be accomplished if growth leaders demanded insight, competencies and capabilities, and a market-driven strategy to navigating risk. This is the uncertainty advantage transformation.

The Landscape of Uncertainty

Creativity is just connecting things. When you ask creative people how they did something, they feel a little guilty because they didn't really do it, they just saw something. It seemed obvious to them after a while. That's because they were able to connect experiences they've had and synthesize new things.

Steve Jobs

What did organizations such as Apple and Cisco do to achieve great success? They executed. They also invested in understanding and navigating uncertainty. Meanwhile, others weighed the benefits and drawbacks of engaging in third-party relationships in far-reaching parts of the world, argued the costs of qualifying multiple suppliers and loss of intellectual property, or turned their heads blindly to the most overt risks. They also recognized the pricing parity issues and the opportunity to lower production and landed costs. However, they failed to reconcile mind-sets, develop the competencies and capabilities, and then aggressively pursue market advantage. The same assertion applies to technology innovation and companies such as JPMorganChase, Starbucks, and Amazon. They not only executed well, they, too, invested heavily in developing the mind-set, competencies, and capabilities necessary in understanding uncertainty. As a result, they gained market advantage. There's a difference between just addressing risk with new operations or initiatives (i.e., delegating it to the managers) and embracing uncertainty as a market differentiator (i.e., embraced by the leaders). For a company in the business of background verification and drug testing, the uncertainty advantage manifested as a decision within forty-eight hours to acquire a competing company and its infrastructure versus limping along over the next several months while trying to rebuild their own infrastructure destroyed after a catastrophic hurricane.

A Market-Driven Point of View

On March 14, 2011, I received a call from the leader of a major hedge fund, the head of research. The call had been prompted by a 9.0 magnitude earthquake and the subsequent tsunami that struck Japan, forty-three miles east of the Oshika Peninsula of Tohoku. An estimated fifteen thousand people lost their lives in this horrific human tragedy. The economic loss was also great, estimated in excess of $365 billion USD.

The conversation began like most. The leader raised questions about the economic and organizational implications of such an event. However, the conversation quickly transitioned away from risk mitigation and recovery to one about the uncertainty competencies and market opportunity. The thesis: uncover investment opportunities that yield significant returns on behalf of the client (market). The hedge fund needed to develop a deeper understanding of flows across multiple tiers and geographies of the supply chain, correlations among industry networks, a map of participants, and inventory levels and cost data (see callout for example). A single source of these data was not available, so the goal was to develop competencies and capabilities and roll up these data to gain an aggregate view that could be continuously monitored for opportunity. While others were trying to minimize the consequences of the event, the hedge fund focused on the landscape of uncertainty strategies.

This is one example of a leader addressing the immediate problem but also looking beyond to spot market advantage made possible by unforeseen events. When large disasters strike, it is only natural to focus on recovery, reduction of further damage, and the most immediate needs. However, uncertainty is not always as immediate and often requires longer-term vision. Just as the hedge fund manager saw two aspects to the catastrophe (the loss of commerce/infrastructure and the separate but important potential it offered), some growth leaders have been able to see beyond the immediate problem to identify a more relevant opportunity it presents.

> It was estimated at the time of the Japan earthquake that Japan produced 16 percent to 30 percent of electronic components for the global market and 50 percent of the supply of semiconductor silicon substrate. The Japanese market was linked to the Taiwanese and Korean markets, as well as the assembly capacity of China. The demand side was global. These industries also closely linked raw materials and chemicals to high-tech manufacturing, with subsequent links to consumer electronics, medical devices, automotive, and energy (to name a few) industries. At the time of the event, 85 percent of the world supply of a critical chemical used in printed circuit boards, bismaleimide triazine (BT) resin, was produced by Mitsubishi Gas Chemical and Hitachi Chemical. Their plants were located in the area impacted by the earthquake. As a result, both suspended production, and the economic quake began. This presented significant opportunity to Taiwanese and other chemical companies that claimed to have created alternative chemicals (Nan Ya Plastics Co. and Elite Materials).[19] The potential opportunities were without boundaries as supply and demand shifted across industries and geographies. This event triggered an uncertainty opportunity in the form of an unplanned change.

---

[16] http://spectrum.ieee.org/semiconductors/memory/how-japans-earthquake-is-shaking-up-taiwans-hightech-sector.

When a leader notices this opportunity, it is a matter of visualizing change as a trigger for moving forward, whether the change is imposed or initiated from the inside.

Every decision has risk and rewards. The purpose of this book is to create opportunities and deliver rewards but to do so by understanding uncertainty, a higher form of risk. Uncertainty and risk both address the unknown. But that's where the similarity ends. Uncertainty describes the unknown, whether it leads to a positive or negative outcome. *Uncertainty is a leadership issue and must be navigated.* Risk, on the other hand, is a probability or threat of damage, injury, liability, loss, or any other negative occurrence caused by external or internal vulnerabilities and that may be avoided through preemptive action.[17] Notice the word "negative"? By design, risk and risk management focus on identifying the best of the worst situations. Even in the world of finance, risk implies a negative as defined in *dictionary.com*, "The probability that an actual return on an investment will be lower than the expected return." Beware! That is the mantra for the current three strategies for managing risk. Other terms used to describe these methods include "value preservation," "resiliency," "inside-out protection," and "compliance." Risk is a management issue and must be managed in the context of performance, compliance/rules, or an adverse event. There is value to each of these strategies, but there are also great limitations when it comes to creating value or engaging leaders responsible for driving growth.

> Prevalent Risk-Based Strategies (note: they are not mutually exclusive)
>
> #1: Threat, Event or Fear, Uncertainty, Doubt (FUD)—a strategy based on strictly reactive methods in which management moves into a defensive posture of cutting losses and limiting exposure.

---

[17] http://www.businessdictionary.com/definition/risk.html#ixzz47nFDgoNFOn.

> #2: Compliance/Rules—the strategic framework based on the regulatory method, whether external (oversight agencies, for example) or internal (corporate governance).
>
> #3: Performance/Asset—strategies based on profitability and preservation of tangible assets; a basic risk-management strategy to uncertainty (e.g., insurance and modeling industries).

In chapter 1, I introduced the market-driven strategy, a fourth strategy rooted in identifying opportunity. In this chapter, I help you to analyze the practical application of the market-driven strategy, recognize the opportunity and how to apply it, and when it should be used. I compare and contrast three traditional strategies of managing risk (threat-based event or FUD based—fear, uncertainty, and doubt; compliance or rules based; and performance/asset-based risk strategies). All have value. However, in contrast, the market-driven strategy begins with an external perspective.

The three traditional strategies begin from within. In other words, the methods, systems, resources, programs, processes, and so on used to support these strategies are defined by the organization and its management (what I refer to as an *inside-out* strategy). The one exception is externally imposed rules and regulations, such as the Sarbanes Oxley Act (US), Gramm-Leach-Bliley Act (US), Solvency II (EU/insurance), Occupational Health and Safety (OSHA), Basel III (Basel Committee on Banking Regulation), HIPAA (Health Insurance Portability and Accountability Act), and/or industry-imposed guidelines. Regulation represents an outside party imposing rules on the industry, organization(s), geography, or topic, but it does not advocate value creation or market advantage. The prior three strategies focus on the manager's top priority of preserving value rather than on the leader's priority of creating growth.

We as an international organizational culture are in the early stages of a market-driven strategy to navigate uncertainty. The early stages of any developing market, technology, or strategy lack clarity, consistency, and widespread acceptance. However, what is consistent is the overwhelming positive reaction and strong desire to engage in conversation by CEOs, directors, and growth leaders representing different markets and geographies. They are frustrated by the limitations of historical risk strategies that do not demonstrate tangible value. This includes existing methods, programs, procedures, technologies, and processes to assess risk and uncertainty. Conversations or questions that mentioned enterprise risk management, compliance, value preservation, risk management, and even strategy risk result in delegation and apathy. Swift but decisive action followed, and the conversation usually is referred to someone in the operations management chain. However, their attitudes and willingness to share practices, strategy, thinking, and experience applying quickly changed when we discussed the topic of navigating uncertainty through a market-driven lens. The discussion engaged and excited many of the growth leaders I either worked with or interviewed.

The Landscape Varies Based on Strategies Employed

Organizations rely on three strategies to manage risk. These all have validity and may be applied in specific situations. They are not mutually exclusive. However, current strategies fail to capture the market driven mindset. Each contains strengths and limitations.

1. Threat-, Event-, or FUD-based (Fear, Uncertainty and Doubt) risk strategy. A common strategy for managing risk and uncertainty, it is often described as firefighting or crisis mode. It is a precise and swift response to a specific disruptive threat or event. Pandemic or epidemics such as Avian Flu (chapter 1), Ebola, and MERS (Middle East Respiratory Syndrome) triggered organizations to immediately adopt a threat based strategy. Not limited to a health crisis other events triggered this strategy included: Brexit, global financial collapse of 2008, Tohoku, Japan earthquake, collapse in oil prices, China stock market

crash, FIFA scandal, terrorist events in London, France, New York, Volkswagen emissions cheating. This strategy is typically supported by relevant crisis communication and management programs, business continuity and emergency response plans, and specific event response scenarios. The bias is to address the specific risk and consequences of the event as quickly as possible and this is accomplished by leveraging the organization's vast resources at the point in time where there is the greatest sense of urgency. The dominant bias is the cognitive bias that the organization and its managers can overcome any challenge via brute force. The goal of this strategy is to smooth volatility, focus on response and resiliency, and do what is necessary to return things to normal. In this mind-set, uncertainty clearly is viewed as a negative force. In addition, an event/threat- or FUD-based strategy attempts to achieve an emotional response, one that is carefully timed to an event (therefore, it is typically tactical and short lived) and used to justify leadership engagement and business investment.

Case: Empire Blue Cross/Blue Shield. There are times when creative solutions arise not only through analysis but also as the result of deep insight. I realized this early in my career with my first exposure to these ideas. The following is my first, and certainly not my last, personal example of a threat-based event and response.

The Serial Killer among Us

My awareness of uncertainty and the potential for large-scale market and customer impact occurred in the late 1970s. Although a very long time ago, it still serves as a threat driven, mind-blowing and rather bizarre example of how management's decisions during moments of cataclysmic uncertainty could accelerate the success or failure of a company, one that had existed for five decades. The urgency in this situation was obvious, and this was another case of an imposed change. I often wonder, though, if the outcome would have been different if it happened in today's mobile-enabled and socially connected world. Today, information spreads rapidly, and all news—especially bad news—is widely known almost instantly.

The year was 1980. I had just accepted my first position in New York City for Blue Cross/Blue Shield (BCBS), one of the largest US health-care insurance providers. I had just begun my job when a Senior Executive ordered me to go to the newsstand on the street and pick up one edition of every major paper. When I returned, he told me to scan the newspapers to see if I could find any stories about a guy named Richard Cottingham. It did not take long. There it was, an event – a trigger - that would define "uncertainty" and whose implications could be felt in the boardroom. Richard Cottingham, as the article indicated, was the name of an accused serial killer. He later became known as the "torso killer."

Although he had murdered and attacked many woman, "Cottingham denied committing any of the murders to the bitter end, despite the fact that some of the victims' property was found in his home and his fingerprint was found on the handcuffs restraining one of the victims. The only thing Cottingham admitted was, 'I have a problem with women.'"[18]

Oh yeah, did I mention that Richard was a night shift operator in our mega data center? This meant Richard had both physical and technical access to more than 30 million customer health and financial records. Management's reaction, keep it quiet, find out what

---

[18] Peter Vronsky, *Serial Killers: The Method and Madness of Monsters,* New York: Berkley Books, 2004, p. xv.

this individual could have possibly done and above all else, do it quickly! As a newly hired and somewhat naïve resource, I became part of the crisis team. The Senior Executive walked me down the hall to a remote office. He inserted his key in the door and there, neatly stacked from floor to ceiling on the light tan carpet in a locked office, were green and white striped computer printouts. Someone had already dumped the system management facility activity logs (referred to as SMF records) in an attempt to better understand all that Richard had done for the last few months.

Suddenly, BCBS's executive management and board would be faced with uncertainty on a scale beyond any they ever imagined, and reaction was urgent. They did not know what might happen or the truth. They lacked the information. The customers' health, personal, and financial records, as well as claim data, were all directly or indirectly available to a privileged user, one who is a night shift operator or manager. The decisions made by the executive team from this point forward would determine whether the organization would be forever distracted from its growth objectives or worst case, be subjected to crippling regulation. It was a different time, and the organization, like most, did not have detailed crisis management, crisis communication, or continuity plans. Fortunately, it appeared that information about the potential concern was contained but we will never know if it had been used for unintended purposes. But what if this individual with privileged access had been doing something else with this sensitive information? It wasn't like we could temporarily turn off the computers. And what about competitors and investors? How would they react and respond if the information had gone social?

If you don't act quickly, your competitors will. BCBS was rightly concerned about the vulnerability this situation created. It needed to get a handle on the company's exposure quickly and at any cost. Urgency dominated management's agenda. Would the competition pounce on the opportunity to gain market share? Would the entire industry be locked down as a result of a systemic breach? Would another business model be created for others to disrupt the traditional health-care insurance model? Would it slow the sales of existing technology platforms and accelerate more secure technology? Would an industry around background checks, breach notifications and employee monitoring spring up? Again, it was a much different time, but suffice to say if it happened today in a heavily regulated industry, operating at Internet speeds, enabled by mobile computing and social media, and with a more sensitized media and general population, the implications and opportunities would be far greater. And so would the opportunities for others!

As it turned out, BCBS dodged that bullet. The case was so bizarre that no blame was assigned to the company.

2. Compliance and rules-driven risk strategy. A compliance- or rules-driven strategy consists of a set of predetermined risk management requirements and a process for complying, often referred to as "checking the box." Typically defined by external entities (government and regulatory; industry, environmental, health, safety groups; business partners and customers via contracts), these requirements are designed as a broad set of minimum requirements and applied to a wide range of participants. The requirements are either mandatory or strongly recommended. Often there are penalties for noncompliance, but many examples involve requirements as mere suggestions. For

many, compliance- and rules-based strategy is perceived as an efficient strategy for striking the balance between doing something and doing nothing while keeping the business profitable (remember the reference in chapter 1 that highlighted the need to analyze your own strategy to managing risk and uncertainty as it might be your greatest exposure). Many of the methods used to support these strategies are qualitative and "unproven" or lack the validation, rigor and repeatability by the scientific, engineering, mathematical, or financial community. Internal rules-based requirements are also included in this strategy. Policies and standards that attempt to eliminate or reduce actions by managers and employees that include preventable risks, internal to an organization, ought to be avoided as unauthorized, illegal, unethical, incorrect, inappropriate actions, and breakdowns in processes. One observation along these lines is

> One danger is that this traditional strategy leads executives to view uncertainty in a binary way—to assume that the world is either certain, and therefore open to precise predictions about the future, or uncertain, and therefore completely unpredictable. Planning or capital-budgeting processes that require point forecasts force managers to bury underlying uncertainties in their cash flows. Such systems clearly push managers to underestimate uncertainty in order to make a compelling case for their strategy.[19]

A word of caution. Several large consulting firms (especially those specializing in audit, tax, compliance, and assurance services) are peddling the concept of strategic risk as an enhancement or next phase of a compliance- or rules-based strategy (e.g., enterprise risk management/ERM program). The good news is that they are linking business

---

[19] Hugh Courtney, Jane Kirkland, and Patrick Viguerie, "Strategy under Uncertainty," *Harvard Business Review*, November 1997.

strategy and innovation to a discussion about risk. The bad news is the way they are defining and recommending action on these risks (illustration 6).

Illustration 4: The COSO ERM Framework

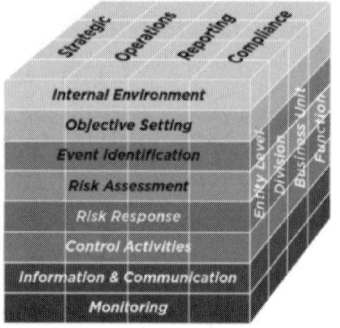

Here's an example of how one firm defines strategy risks: "those risks that threaten to disrupt the assumptions at the core of an organization's strategy."[20] The article goes on to describe these risks as everything from black swans to political upheavals. From a manager's perspective, especially a manager of risk or compliance, it helps to think about the events and what-if scenarios. However, from a market and leadership perspective, it's unclear as to what specific executable actions should be taken or whether these disruptive forces may create an opportunity. From a practical standpoint, adopting a strategy that throws caution and risk in the way of potential growth is never a good starting point, especially if you are trying to engage or incentivize the growth leader.

---

[20] "Deloitte CFO Insights: Facing (and Embracing) Strategic Risks," *CFO Innovation*, February 1, 2016.

3. Performance/asset-based risk strategy. Performance/asset-based strategies have been used in the field of financial risk management for many years and is the most recent trend in operational and supply/value chain risk management. The financial risk methods include value at risk (VaR), profit at risk, conditional value at risk (CVaR), and many others. As it applies to markets and operations, the recent uptick in interest has been to tie the impacts to investment or allocation of large risk mitigation and financing efforts. The goal is to measure risk return on investment in the same context that operational efficiency is measured (e.g. margin, inventory turns). Performance-based risk strategy currently resides within the operations.

Illustration 5: Risk to Performance Based Modeling

Expected Sales Per Month	318,750,000	
	Randomized Number of Break Points	
	1 Break Point	2 Break Points
Average Sales Lost in %	2.95%	6.27%
Average Sales Lost in $	375,718,275	798,968,550
Worst Case Lost in %	28.00%	44.37%
Worst Case Lost in $	3,570,038,250	5,657,396,850
0% Fill Rate More than 6 Months %	8.83%	17.31%
Average Sales Lost above 6 Months	121,144,125	239,916,750

Average Sales Lost in $
375,718,275 — 1 Break Point
798,968,550 — 2 Break Points

Worst Case Lost in $
3,570,038,250 — 1 Break Point
5,657,396,850 — 2 Break Points

In all of these strategies, the major item excluded is the market (customers, investors, strategic partners, regulators, community, etc.). The uncertainty advantage is a practical application of leadership, and all of the cases I present in this book make that point repeatedly.

What Is Meant by a "Value-Driven Process"?

The word 'process' has been overused to describe any number of organizational activities. In terms of value, however, we can fine-tune this word to clarify its meaning. A "value driven process" is not merely a function or routine; it is intentionally designed to create positive market growth outcomes, especially when exploiting uncertainty that is found in all initiatives.

The value driven process is a discipline to create and foster efficiency, and to accomplish well-defined strategic goals. In this sense, value driven outcomes, according to many, become assets in their own right – not tangible assets like desks and autos, but process-related assets of great value. [21]

My interview with Francois Nader made this point as well as put the risk to performance strategy in perspective.

> He explained that physical events are the easy part, but decisions and behaviors are a different matter. "My focus was to double check, and validate the data." This is as fine a definition of a value-driven process as any other. Nader continued: "Other aspect that I apply personally include the values of company, its culture. At NPS as a physician you put patients at the center, it's the core of everything you do. If you couple the patient and value than decision making is very clear. For me if the values include integrity, it is a very binary thing for me. It either works or it doesn't work."[22]

Nader expressed a clear set of priorities in his vision, and demonstrated how his value-driven approach to issues worked. He went on to say, "It's a continuum, I have to take risk and the bar is set by patients, markets and regulators. Once you make decisions that are within the moral boundaries (don't cheat, steal, etc.) then every day I have to take calculated risks in everything I do. My gut feel is not always correct. It's influenced by a number of short term factors. I always try to look at

---

[21] Peter Franz and Mathias Kirchmer, *Value-Driven Business Process Management*. New York: McGraw-Hill, 2012.

[22] Author's interview with Francois Nader, Board Chairman, Acceleron Pharma (XLRN); Board Director, Baxalta (BXLT) and Clementia; Former President and CEO, NPS Pharma.

things from a metrics and performance perspective, but I acknowledge that the data can say whatever you want. The challenge is not looking at the numbers but rather *it's validating the numbers with our judgements.* What I find fascinating is a model that tells me that there is a 70% probability that the drug will be approved. But the approval of the drug is binary. It either goes through or not. In the end I uncertainty is defined as either the drug is going to make it or is not going to make it.

Like many growth leaders, his situation-driven leadership style set him apart. But this raises additional questions relating to priority-setting in an environment of uncertainty.

In all of these strategies, the major item excluded is the *Markets* (customers, investors, strategic partners, regulators, community, etc.). The Uncertainty Advantage is a practical application of leadership, and a recurring theme in all of the cases I present in this book make that point repeatedly.

These strategies can be compared when placed on a graph, with the identifying attributes used to describe how they function and how they differ. Illustration 6 compares the four strategies and lays out the two axis of each.

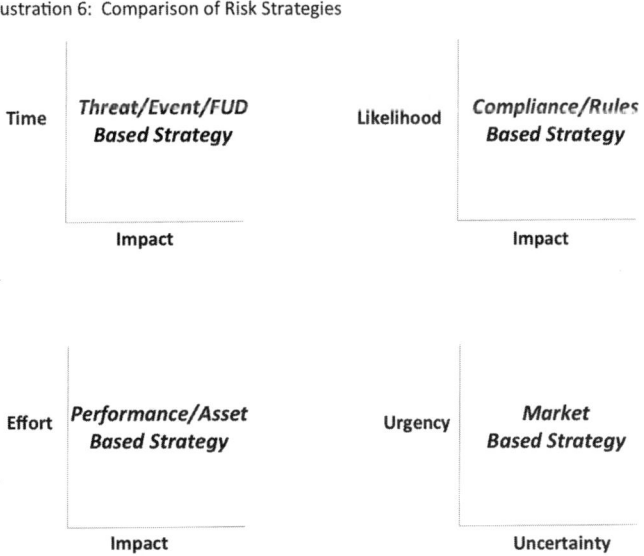

Illustration 6: Comparison of Risk Strategies

Change as a Trigger

Change is the catalyst and the trigger to engage the uncertainty advantage mind-set and the first element of the "situation." As previously described in chapter 1, the "situation" represents the priority at a point in time and includes: the change, opportunity, expected outcomes, decisions, and uncertainty. Change can materialize in many ways, so we will need to be acutely aware of how to detect it at the onset, when change first occurs. There are two types of changes to consider, imposed and initiated.

1. Imposed change. When events occur, you typically have no control over them. This requires you to make critical business decisions and understand the uncertainty involved. Typically, this is for the purpose of minimizing the negative consequences of change. However, the market focus is on exploiting the opportunity. The Hyundai example illustrates this type of economic change.

2. Initiated change. When you decide there's an opportunity for your organization, you initiate change. Outsourcing, mergers, business design, and other such changes are examples. A thorough understanding of uncertainty is essential to the result. This also leads to more precise decisions. The hedge fund example previously described in this chapter illustrates an initiated change.

Illustration 7: Types of Change

The hedge fund manager reacted to the earthquake with a two-part mind-set. First was the element of recovery as a priority; second was recognition of the opportunity that was created as a result. Even when a disaster does not occur, a threat to an operation's existence can bring about just as dramatic a change. One such case was that of the remarkable odyssey of Intel.

An Innovative Growth Leader—Intel

Andy Grove, CEO of Intel and ultimate growth leader, transformed the company into the largest global producer of semiconductors. That, by itself, was impressive, but the way it happened is far more interesting and instructive. This is an interesting case because Grove first realized a change was being imposed via market evolution and then identified a way a change could become advantageous.

Grove learned about integrated circuitry in the 1960s when he was assistant director of development at Fairchild Semiconductor. This led years later to a revolution in microprocessing. In 1968, Grove left Fairchild and joined the newly formed Intel as director of engineering. Intel at that time was focused on producing and marketing memory chips, or DRAMs (dynamic random access memory).

By 1976, market uncertainty began to escalate as demand started falling off as a result of Japanese companies dumping memory chips onto the market below cost. Grove realized that the memory chip market was no longer a successful product for Intel, so he suggested a radical change, moving from chips to the semiconductor business. This "defining" phase was characterized by change, opportunity, and uncertainty on many levels. Should Intel abandon the DRAM business altogether? Would semiconductor production succeed for the long term? What was the competition? These questions pointed to the urgency of the situation. The landscape was changing before Intel's eyes. Andy Grove described these as "inflection points." So their choice was to figure out how to make their original product cheaper or make a drastic change. Failing either of these, they would be forced out of business.

Moving from a known and established market into an entirely new one was risky, but Grove saw that the entire market was changing. The supply side had to respond to movement on the demand side (the market), moving away from the company's only business. Grove recognized the coming change and was determined to be the leader in this new microprocessing industry. It was time to act. This consisted of converting uncertainty into market advantage. He was a key negotiator in convincing IBM to place Intel microprocessors in all their person computers, the now well-known "Intel inside."

It was not an easy decision. Grove described the transformation he and Intel's CEO shared and how they came to the decision to move forward and, essentially, change their own landscape.

> I remember a time in the middle of 1985, after this aimless wandering had been going on for almost a

year. I was in my office with Intel's chairman and CEO, Gordon Moore, and we were discussing our quandary. Our mood was downbeat. I looked out the window at the Ferris wheel of the Great America amusement park revolving in the distance, then I turned back to Gordon and I asked, "If we got kicked out and the board brought in a new CEO, what do you think he would do?" Gordon answered without hesitation, "He would get us out of memories." I stared at him, numb, then said, "Why shouldn't you and I walk out the door, come back and do it ourselves?"[23]

By 1997, Intel's revenues had grown to $20.8 billion, versus its first-year revenue of only $2,672. During Grove's time as CEO, market cap of Intel grew by 4,500 percent, from $4 billion to $197 billion. Intel grew to become the seventh-largest corporation in the world.[24]

In the case of Intel, the primary market was being crushed by Japanese companies underselling the market. This created a reactionary form of uncertainty management. The market was no longer working, so what could Intel do about it?

This story turned proactive at this point and uncertainty would soon be viewed through an opportunity lens. Not only did Intel invent a new market and product for itself, they recognized how uncertainty could be transformed. The turning point was negotiating with IBM to include "Intel inside" in all their computers. They also successfully reconciled the leader and manager mind-sets. For example, Andy Grove went to Oregon, Intel's most modern memory chip plant, gathered the managers, and spoke about "Welcome to the mainstream." Grove described their reaction as follows.

---

[23] Andrew S. Grove, *"Only the Paranoid Survive: How to Exploit the Crisis Points That Challenge Every Company"*, Doubleday, 1999

[24] "1997 Technology Leader of the Year Andy Grove: Building an Information Age Legacy," *IndustryWeek.com*, December 15, 1997; Andrew Nocera, "From Intel to Health Care and Beyond," *The New York Times*, July 30, 2005.

I said that Intel's mainstream was going to be microprocessors. By signing up to do microprocessor development, they would be bearing the flag for Intel's mainline business.

It actually went a lot better than I had expected. These people, like our customers, had known what was inevitable before we in senior management faced up to it. There was a measure of relief that they no longer had to work on something that the company wasn't fully committed to. This group, in fact, threw itself into microprocessor development and they have done a bang-up job ever since.

How would an operations or financial manager have treated this situation? Without the vision and strategy risk mind-set and the ability to initiate change, the idea of getting out of a primary business altogether would be unthinkable. However, that was the only solution that made sense. In this case, a reactive form of uncertainty management grew from an unexpected event (like being undercut by price strategy in the market). Proactivity is a form of uncertainty management that creates a strategy and new markets, products, or strategic domination of a market sector.

As a well-known celebrity once said,

> "Life is about not knowing, having to change, taking the moment and making the best of it, without knowing what's going to happen next."[25]

That brings us to our next key concept—uncertainty navigation (versus managing uncertainty or the management of risk). To navigate is to lead, to take risk, learn, fail fast, adjust or adapt, and go forward. To navigate is to understand and embrace uncertainty. John Rockefeller,

---

[25] Gilda Ratner, quoted in www.values.com/inspirational-quotes.

J. P. Morgan, Andrew Carnegie, Steve Jobs, Sam Walton, Ray Kroc, Larry Ellison, Howard Schultz, Richard Branson, Jack Welch, Jeff Bezos, Marvin Bower, and so many other great leaders all welcomed and leveraged uncertainty. They evangelized the mind-set by demanding that their leaders possess the competencies and develop the capabilities to transform this valuable asset and market differentiator.

Navigating uncertainty includes Andy Grove's paranoia and clear vision; Jack Welch's persistence, relentlessness, and focus; Steve Job's ability to create an unexplored emotional experience; Howard Schultz's humility, willingness to take risks, and ability to create shared value over individual benefits (more about this in chapter 4). A boundary-free market that creates shared value is an incubator of positive thinking and creativity, which roots out unnecessary risks while augmenting opportunity.

Now you understand the opportunity and the choices. After this comes the question of when and what to apply. In the next chapter, I challenge you to imagine a new transformation agenda for acting as a growth leader and transforming your organization as well as your personal mind-set.

The Transformation Agenda

The transformation agenda is your higher plain of action within an uncertain environment, your vision, and your road map for execution when change occurs. It's a growth leader's visual that describes the end game and the path to navigate and transform the uncertainty advantage mind-set. It's a manager's path to value enablement and engagement. What is needed? As long as the transformation agenda is the starting point, leaders, managers, and markets can reconcile their priorities and agree on the same destination. What is new about this? Too many organizations attempt to transform without reconciliation and the mental model. The uncertainty advantage changes all of that.

A Personal Transformation: Outside-In View from an Inside-Out Experience

In my career, I have gone through a series of realizations and transformations. I witnessed where traditional risk management makes sense and where it does not. I observed that leaders and managers are like Mars and Venus or growth and performance. At one point in my career, I truly believed that leaders didn't care about risk or uncertainty, and that managers did (correction, *some* managers). However, the fact is leaders care as much as the opportunity it presents, but you have to ask the right questions.

My first book, *At Your Own Risk: How the Risk-Conscious Culture Meets the Challenge of Business Change* (Wiley, 2008), reflected this thinking. My second book, *Single Point of Failure: The 10 Essential Laws of Supply Chain Risk Management* (Wiley, 2009), represented this transformation from previous threat-driven and rules-based strategy to a performance-driven strategy. This book clearly focuses on the next wave of the transformation: the market-driven strategy to navigating uncertainty. Prior risk strategies satisfied the needs of senior-most management (and the auditors, regulators), but not the growth leaders. When I presented performance-based results and solutions to clients, their focus was not on performance but on the market, future growth, and anything that might get in its way.

After several years of perfecting a performance driven strategy to understanding risk and uncertainty in complex supply chains (I referred to it as a "value" based strategy), I uncovered an opportunity to leverage newly developed uncertainty competencies and capabilities and convert them into a new supply chain insurance product (more about this case in chapter 6). The "value" based strategy had been deployed at organizations in the hi-tech, industrial manufacturing, pharmaceutical, energy and chemical industry. After several years of applying the strategy one of our growth leaders at Marsh suggested we explore leveraging our knowledge of uncertainty to create a new product and revenue stream. Along with other leaders (underwriters, business developers, product owners), managers (operations, technology, legal), and the market (customers, investors, regulators), we reconciled our individual mind-sets, leveraged our competencies and capabilities, and collectively had created a new product and revenue stream.

In all cases presented throughout this book, growth leaders seeking market advantage asked similar questions as they embarked on change for a specific situation or opportunity.

- What is the business opportunity ("situation") and the uncertainty ahead?
- Does it alter my expectations, or does it create new ones?
- What competencies and capabilities are needed or do I need to invest in to thoroughly understand and potentially leverage uncertainty (within an allowable time period and effort)?
- To what degree has the industry competitors, investors, strategic partners, and regulators thought or acted on this opportunity?
- What are my competitor's and strategic partner's mind-sets, capabilities, and competencies?

This new breed of innovative leaders internalized, embraced, and exploited every opportunity that uncertainty presented. It wasn't by accident, and their advances reflected a different mind-set. They quickly developed or tapped into capabilities and competencies at least as fast as they were introducing and acting on change. Their questions about uncertainty demanded the collection of more robust data, greater subject matter expertise, understanding of not only their business model but that of others, and a mind-set that focused on understanding the market first—competitors, customers, investors, strategic partners, and regulators. What I observed was the beginning of a market-driven strategy to navigate, not manage, uncertainty, one defined by the potential for creating value, not preserving it. Jeffrey Immelt, CEO of General Electric, best summed up today's business climate during his commencement speech at Siena College. He proclaimed that

> The margin for opportunity and error is smaller than ever before. This is a world where the only certainty is unpredictability and change.

As I mentioned earlier, I'm not suggesting that past strategies for managing risk and uncertainty should be abandoned. Quite the contrary. What I present are examples of the limitations and lack of reconciliation of prior thinking, strategies, systems, programs, and methods for managing risk and not embracing uncertainty. The market-driven transformation has just begun.

As a growth leader, your destination is clearly defined as unattainable. The end just doesn't exist. Your goal is predictable, sustainable, and continuous growth. You never reach the destination because if you did, you would cease to exist in today's hypercompetitive markets. Let's face it, the market will always raise the bar, and although risk and uncertainty are important, they're not as important as your ability to survive and thrive. As a leader, this is your fundamental operating assumption. However, as a manager, your goals are a bit clearer, often quantifiable, and expressed as metrics or key performance indicators (KPIs). They are derived from the organization's goals—for example, gross margin—and expressed in terms of the individual manager or function. This provides tangible and achievable metrics in the context of the overall performance goal (e.g., return on assets, inventory turns).

However, when this same approach is applied to measure risk, the results are quite different. They tend to be soft, qualified metrics supported by what appears to be never-ending assessments. Expressed in terms of impact, the visual is usually a checklist, heat map, or stoplight (red, yellow, green) charts. This is true of existing risk management strategies and associated programs (FUD/threat-, compliance/rules-, and performance/asset-based), but not so of the market-driven strategy to navigating uncertainty. These goals are defined by the market and can be either quantified or qualified, usually a combination of both. They are clear and concise. Let's review the goals of the market-driven strategy as outlined in chapter 1.

- Create new revenue/growth opportunity.
- Improve performance via efficiency in the allocation of risk resources (time, management focus, capital/budget, people/talents).
- Establish market advantage via faster, better, more accurate decision-making; provide greater market confidence and trust.

A market-driven strategy requires a change in mind-set, but the transformation agenda is not an isolated process or program. Nor is it a complex, large-scale or multi-million dollar change program that requires massive redeployment of internal resources or armies of consultants. It is an adjustment, an adaptation, an expansion to the growth leader's current thinking about change and critical decisions. It should be simple and natural in the context of growth savvy and execution. So the transformation agenda must closely parallel a growth leader's existing thought process and behaviors (gut, instinct, values) in order for the leader to accept, internalize, adopt, and promote the strategy and principles. It must be simple, relevant, and aligned with the individual's motivations and incentives. This is not an easy task, but actions are predicated on enhanced market-focused outcomes such as market advantage, efficiencies, greater trust, speed, and confidence. The following highlights attributes of a market-driven strategy for navigating uncertainty to the other three risk strategies. As you can see by the comparison, the market-driven strategy (uncertainty advantage) is simple, defined by the market, personal, situational, linked to change, and tied directly the important decisions. It can be applied in the context of your everyday pursuit of growth and decision-making. Most important, for sustainability and a bit of a reality check, it not only defines a strategy (in the business context) but also outlines what's needed to execute. The principles included in the strategy reflect the learning from ten years of cases, discussions, and research.

Comparison of Strategies: Market-Based versus Threat/Event/FUD-Based, Compliance or Rules-Based, Performance-Based Strategies

Key Issue	Market-Based Strategy	Risk-Based Strategies (Threat, Compliance, Performance)
What triggers action—when to execute?	Change trigger (imposed or initiated)	Planned/scheduled (reactive for threats being realized)

Key Issue	Market-Based Strategy	Risk-Based Strategies (Threat, Compliance, Performance)
Who owns/drives?	Leader	Manager (usually by function)
What is the basis of the strategy, that is, its main purpose?	Create value	Preserve value
What is the context for applying?	Situation	Organization (broad, sweeping application)
What is the uncertainty advantage strategy through execution premise?	Navigate	Manage
What is the uncertainty advantage navigation principle?	Market	Performance, threat/FUD, compliance/rules
What is the uncertainty advantage navigation principle?	Growth priority	Risk-centric
What is the uncertainty advantage navigation principle?	Urgency	Planned and scheduled
What is the uncertainty advantage navigation principle?	Detail-oriented	Generalization, wide application

In an interview with Karen Avery, a Partner with PriceWaterhouseCoopers and career business risk strategist (Marsh & McLennan, GE Capital, JPMorgan), she described a transformation that had just begun for a multi-billion dollar global enterprise.

> In recent years the conversations with CEOs, CFOs and senior executives have been about bringing greater value to risk investments. No longer were these conversations driven by the need to do something but rather it was about doing that something well, something that provided tangible value to the priorities of the business and the market served. The conversation was also not about

taking on less risk and imposing greater governance or control but rather it was about going faster, uncovering ways to take on more risk while staying in front of the market and competition. However, this theme did not always ring true when talking with senior risk professionals (Chief Risk Officer, Compliance Director, Enterprise Risk Manager, Regulatory Executive, General Auditor). The initial conversation was almost always about the risk executive explaining how they would like to be more relevant and provide greater value to the business leaders. They used words like tangible, inclusive, embedded (in the business and market strategy as well at the onset of the business decision making process). They wanted to go beyond implementing a large, multi-year corporate program, providing checklists, conducting assessments, verifying remediation efforts, and a contributing to a defensive strategy.

For example, I had a risk strategy conversation with the executives of a European-based global manufacturing organization. They explained how they had spent a lot of money on their Enterprise Risk Management (ERM) Program; however, they struggled to justify their investment. Their Head of Corporate Strategy and Head of ERM both wanted to know how they could improve risk management within the company. The program was compliant with many of today's industry standards; however, they felt that it was expensive and not connected well with business strategy. The business sector leaders did not see a need or benefit to engage the risk executives early in the decision making process. They observed that risk management executives were not engaging in business conversations around macro trends, industry trends, the specific initiative, and disruptive forces in the markets. As a result, the risk executive had little ability to contribute and the investment lacked significant "value."

To address the disconnect, we decided to take a step back and look at the CEO's and investor's market aspirations. What was the multi-year plan for business growth and innovation? What markets were most important? It turned out that the CEO of the organization made it painfully clear that he wanted the organization to (1) align their businesses around three strategic trends and opportunities, (2) cut cost—not for the sake of cutting cost but rather to reduce distractions and improve efficiency in what they did best, and (3) reinvest the savings in initiatives that matter most in the market, to their customers and to future performance. The Head of Corporate Strategy and the CFO recommended that the ERM program be used as a case for realignment, reinvestment and innovative, value creation. After all, from a risk perspective the ERM program investment was one of the organization's most visible, expensive, pervasive, and problem programs. This would require deeper intelligence and insight into industry and business trends, the opportunity, business expectations and critical decisions, and risk and the opportunities that could be created from possessing greater insight, capabilities and data.

What we were discussing was the need to return to the originally intended purpose of risk (and the business!). Originally, professionals engaged in risk activities to maximize the return on investment, despite volatility. Over the years as risk management expanded and moved beyond financial services organizations, it took on a life of its own with large expensive multi-year programs, functional behaviors, rules and restrictions, greater governance, and extraordinary oversight by regulators. Risk, compliance, regulatory, audit, and program investments ballooned. The value question, i.e. what is the value of the risk investment, rang louder and louder as investments grew and time passed. The programs became so big that the organization lost site of the original purpose of risk, which was to support the business in its effort to create value in the marketplace, make money, invest wisely, and make better decisions.

How does the Risk Executive get back to basics and connect with the business in terms of strategy? First, when thinking about risk, start with the market and work inward. Outside-in versus inside-out. Engage in deep conversations about business expectations and opportunities and industry/geography and market research to understand where the organization operates today and in the future. Next, identify significant macro and industry trends relevant to the industry, organization, geography, and market to better understand the opportunities and uncertainties. Take the time to identify and understand customers, competitors, regulators, investors requirements and behaviors. Finally, leverage and develop new capabilities in order to take advantage of opportunities including situational based thinking, scenario analysis (in terms of opportunity), risk sensing techniques, behavioral analysis, data and analytics, and deeper business acumen.

The Transformation

Initially, I avoided naming what I am about to describe. Why? Let's just say after serving years as an industry practitioner (the buy side), market analyst (the outside in), and management consultant (the supply side), I detest the use of buzz or buzzwords to describe the latest craze. So

I've decided to keep it simple and describe it as the UTA or uncertainty transformation agenda. What's important here is not the name but, rather, the integrating of the concepts and process into your natural leader or manager thought process.

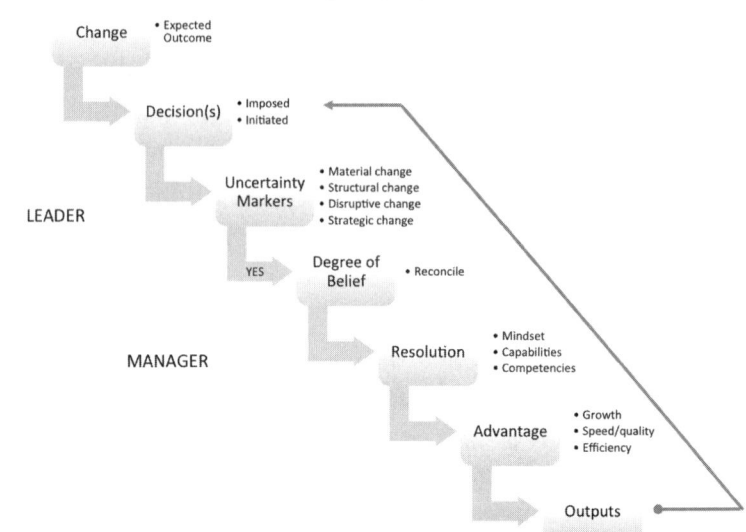

Illustration 8: Uncertainty Transformation Agenda (UTA)

UTA is a visual of the transformation agenda. A case study is used to describes how the UTA drives a market driven strategy. An explanation of key terms, concepts and processes follow the case study.

Case Study: Multinational Global Leader of Consumer Products

Change was initiated by growth leaders supported by the managers of a $7 billion multinational world leader in the consumer products industry. The organization had been on an acquisition spree, expanding its North American presence and as a result found itself operating seventeen warehouses and distribution centers that shipped more than 110 million products annually. The change consisted of an optimization initiative in order to achieve greater efficiency and consistent, scalable, and superior levels of service. As you might expect, the cost of doing business and level of service varied by location for moving the product. The cost basis ranged from as high as $32 to a low of less than one dollar. The growth leader, supported by the managers, engaged a management consultant to run the optimization models and another to provide specialized knowledge (competency and capabilities) into uncertainty and conduct a business risk analysis. The managers assumed the output would confirm their belief that there would be a gain of more than $3 million if they consolidated from seventeen distribution centers to one mega-distribution center. The leaders did not express the same level of confidence and instead wanted those with a deep understanding of uncertainty to challenge the assumptions and run the numbers. The management team believed that in addition to a $3 million gain in performance that they could provide adequate resiliency for the mega-center. They believed that in the event of a major disruption that they could restore the mega-center in less than 7 weeks. The uncertainty consultants, while conducting the analysis and attempting to validate the $3 million, uncovered an enormous potential market disadvantage. They estimated the market exposure of a major disruption to be $230 million annually. They also determined that there would be almost 100 percent loss of independent labs and a need to competitively source their owned labs. The leaders were correct to challenge the managers understanding of uncertainty. In defense of the managers, unsubstantiated assumption and performance based biases are not uncommon. The need to reconcile leaders, managers and market mind-sets became apparent. As a result, changes were made to the model, adding a second or third distribution center and reallocating the fill rates. The location and information about uncertainty about the location (augmented by property and hazard modelers) was added to the analysis. The new model reflected exposure had been reduced from $230 million to $17 million annually, a substantial drop. The recovery time in the event of a shutdown was also reduced from fifty-six weeks to four to six weeks. The process included analysis at the micro-level with the questions, If a particular distribution goes down, how long will it take to get back up? and, do our competitors understand uncertainty at this level, and what have they done to address market exposure?

Ironically, while working on the assignment, one of their competitors experienced a devastating fire at one of their major plants in the Asia-Pacific region. Their competitor was forced to source from them, providing strategic market advantage.

A result of this examination was the discovery that many of the previously set assumptions about the time and cost for recovery efforts were inaccurate and heavily biased. The organization selected a second distribution center. This provided an added market advantage of enabling the company to allocate the mix of products in each center based on regional location of customers and mix of business by region. Diversifying the supplier distribution network diversified risk and also created market advantage in greater efficiency of distribution itself. They team had optimized the performance of the distribution network, thus improving margins while optimizing resiliency, thus providing efficient allocation of risk resources and greater market confidence.

In this case, growth was recognized as an essential aspect of business, but in the process of growing, risk levels had grown as well. Does an organization live with that added risk? Do they apply traditional risk management processes to the supply chain? Or do they act as the organization did and analyze the problem to facilitate growth while reducing disruption risk?

UTA: Deeper Dive

- *Situation:* As previously stated, the "situation" is the growth leader context. It includes a specific change, opportunity, expectations, assumptions, decisions, and uncertainty. It's what matters most to the growth leader, organization and ultimately the market.

    o *Case:* Recent expansion of the business via acquisition presented opportunity to gain efficiencies thus improving margins and competitive position.

- *Change* (the trigger)—The "situation" arises due to change, whether it is self-initiated or imposed. Change acts as the trigger and is what creates uncertainty. Examples of change include: actions by activists or regulators; significant foreign exchange or commodity volatility; legal/statutory/regulatory actions; mergers, acquisitions, divestures, outsourcing, new entrants, near-sourcing; structural change in the industry; technology innovation or disruption; pandemics and epidemics; terrorism; fire, floods, earthquakes, and so on. Change as the trigger—too often, we tend to think of change as a negative force within the organization. The truth is, nothing worth doing occurs without change. Nothing happens, in fact, without uncertainty, and uncertainty is always accompanied by change, often in big ways. The concept of linking in the thinking process to change in order to choose a strategy is crucial to the transformation process. Without this linkage, we have no way to know where we are going. It all begins with the trigger of change.

  o *Case:* As a result of on an acquisition spree, creating seventeen warehouses and distribution centers that shipped more than 110 million products annually, change was initiated by the organization to eliminate redundancy and improve financial performance.

- *Expected Business Outcome*—For an initiated change, the desired/possible output or expectation (e.g., percentage of market expansion, increase in revenue, reduction in margin, etc.). It is what is the growth leader believes the opportunity from change will yield. For an imposed change, it is the growth leader's initial assessment of the impact or expected outcomes from change. Bottom line, there must be a defined expectation and/or benefit for the investment.

  o *Case:* a gain of more than $3 million if they consolidated from seventeen distribution centers to one mega-distribution center. However, the performance gain would immediately be wiped out and the brand severely damaged if the mega-center was disrupted for and extended period.

- *Decision(s)*—Situational decisions are the critical business decisions that the growth leader needs to make to achieve the expected outcomes. It includes the assumptions about what it will take to realize the opportunity and may be expressed as a hypothesis, statement, or assertion. As pointed out in the book, Blue Ocean Strategy,[26] a different context may be needed. For the uncertainty advantage, I suggest the context be presented in terms of business change and the situation rather than trying to apply a broad-based strategy across the entire organization as part of some grandiose transformation strategy. The author made reference to, "There are no permanent excellent companies. We do smart and not so smart things. We study what we did that was positive, our strategic moves. We use different unit of measure, the context is the situation." . For example, "To achieve a 4 percent increase in gross margin, we will need to consolidate the distribution network." The output of UTA is to provide more succinct input to the decision process and to modify the original assumptions for accuracy or opportunity where appropriate.

  o *Case:* Decision focused on how to gain a $3 million cost saving and transition from seventeen distribution centers to one without disrupting the customer experience. How many distribution centers? Where should they be located? What should the product mix/fill rates be? What level of resiliency do the different models provide? What do our

---

[26] W. Chan Kim and Renee Mauborgne, *"Blue Ocean Strategy, How to Create Uncontested Market Space and Make the Competition Irrelevant"* (Harvard Business Review Press, expanded edition, January 20, 2015).

competitors do? How prepared are they for disruption, and is there and opportunity?

- *Uncertainty*—The unknown about the situational change (assumptions, impacts, effects, consequences) is, by definition, uncertain. In fact, nothing is certain. There is always some element or factor that could change outcomes. Typically, risk methods (e.g., probabilistic, deterministic, etc.) are applied to help predict or determine the potential outcomes and to facilitate the decision by choosing the best of the worst outcomes. Risk programs are developed and implemented to support best practices and behaviors for reducing the impact or, in some instances, the likelihood. Uncertainty has obstacles and opportunities. These so-called obstacles challenge the management agenda by consuming resources that would normally be suited to support the business agenda (and expected performance). Precious resources such as time, management attention, capital/budget, and staff/skills must be carefully allocated to achieve performance targets. But what if we knew more about uncertainty than our competitors? What if we could clearly demonstrate the value in understanding uncertainty to our investors or strategic partners? What if we were able to uncover an opportunity to be materially more accurate when undertaking change, investing in an opportunity and making critical business decisions or assumptions?

- *Uncertainty Advantage Markers*—Key indicators established by the growth leader and/or organization can qualify the change as having the potential for material, strategic, structural, transformational, and market positioning impact (i.e., it's worth the investment). The change directly impacts the growth leader's agenda and provides the opportunity to gain market advantage (e.g., new growth opportunity, greater precision to decisions or faster execution, improved performance, reduction of total risk for a given expected return). Examples include those changes that are material to the business strategy/plan; strategic, material, long-range financial or market impact; significant market and/or technology disrupters; and new entrants or technology to the market. The market and managers' mind-sets (beliefs and biases) must be profiled and incorporated into the process. One of the three other strategies (threat/FUD, compliance/rules, performance/asset) is applied if the change does not meet the predefined criteria.

  o *Case:* Customer segment was represented by several hundred company-owned laboratories as well as independent labs. Investor segment represented via status as a publicly traded company. Managers were biased toward the one mega-center concept. They believed that they could manage any disruption and have the center back up in four to six weeks. The study revealed that the actual recovery time was fifty-six weeks. Competencies and capabilities needed; gain thorough understanding of the distribution network and flow of materials, products, cash, and information (competency). Mapped interoperability and interrelationships of other network flows (competency). Leveraged failure mode effect (FMEA) data for the top ten product lines (capabilities). Analyzed fill rates for top product lines/SKUs (competencies). Modeled uncertainty as it applied to different assumptions and scenarios (competencies).

- *Degree of Belief*—Each of the major stakeholders (market, growth leader, manager) has a level of confidence in the hypothesis (stated/believed business outcome derived from the imposed or initiated change). Why do leaders and managers constantly request assessments, typically by independent parties? To either validate or improve their degrees of belief in their assumptions (or in other instances, as we will see in the TRUMPF business case in chapter 4, to tell them what they don't know). However, the uncertainty could be a potential opportunity, but the assessment must be conducted from a market point of view. This requires knowledge of what the market desires, not just what the leaders and managers suggest. The first great challenge is reconciliation of the mind-set and appetite (perhaps more often called "risk appetite") for each of the three major actors. Markets, leaders, and managers will rarely be in complete agreement about outcomes and expectations, so these have to be developed into a single, agreed set. To resolve uncertainty, what do we need? Greater insight requires application of competencies and capabilities. Biases will prevent moving forward, so as part of your task, you need to identify and confront these and decide how to replace them with unbiased and shared interests. These biases stem from fear, selective hearing, bullying, brute force, wishful thinking, filtered or biased information, or emotions (overinvestment). Reconcile various beliefs, biases, and appetites. Ultimately, the growth leader or senior-most executive will make the final decision.

- *The Clock and Calendar*—The clock is always running, defining the urgency of your initiative; and the calendar is forever moving forward, a measure of timing for execution. As so many examples have revealed, many companies have recognized the key ingredient of transforming uncertainty into market advantage: If you do not act on uncertainty, it will act on you. The two forces of uncertainty and urgency work hand in hand. When faced with uncertainty, a first impulse is to stop, watch, and ponder. This is a mistake. The relentless pursuit of the cause and effect underlying uncertainty is the requirement when facing uncertainty. Of course, this assumes that you possess a real-time understanding of the core issues at work and that you are able to monitor trends and filter through the noise that invariably accompanies uncertainty.

- *Resolution*—What's needed to resolve uncertainty and uncover uncertainty market opportunity?

    o *Competencies*: Competencies and skills are required as part of this plan. They have to be identified and folded into your growth leadership plan. In coming chapters, I provide examples of how growth leaders accomplished this. However, competencies grow not only from experience but also from gut instinct.

    o Capabilities: Every individual and every organization has limits, but they also need to understand the full extent of what they can do, not only what they cannot do. Positive thinking based on reality is a powerful method. Forms and examples of capabilities include,

        1. Methods—Resilient, precise, robust, and proven methods are needed to determine and measure uncertainty. These may be scientific-, mathematic-, economic-, and engineering-based methods that have been publicly vetted.

        2. Data and Data Sources—These must be diverse, consistent, reliable, timely, and predictive sources, including signal, sensing, and listening posts.

        3. Allocation Strategy—Simple and precise methods to allocate a portfolio of solutions, forms of mitigation, financing, and avoidance of threats. This is a performance-based strategy that still works within the market-driven strategy.

        4. Behavioral Analysis—Often overlooked is the importance of insight and analytics to understanding and

anticipating how behavior influences and impacts uncertainty, not to mention predictability.

5. Processes and Programs—Formalized, efficient strategic processes and programs must be directly relevant to each situation.

6. Visualization—There must be the ability to create a picture that will influence the market mind-set and communicate visually through animations, images, Figures, and diagrams.

   o *Case:* Guidance included recommendations for optimal fill rates for each center based on a model developed (competency and capability) that optimizes efficiency and resiliency simultaneously.

- *Advantage*—Market differentiation, leverage, and outputs must be scrutinized. On completion of the analysis, leverage competencies and/or capabilities to uncover opportunity. Incorporate into original business decision. Create new revenue/growth opportunity, improve performance via efficiency in the allocation of risk resources (time, management focus, capital/budget, people/talents), or establish market advantage via faster, better, more accurate decision-making. Provide greater market confidence and trust.

   o *Case:* Efficient design optimized for disruptions provides greater resiliency and market confidence. Expectations adjusted to reflect a more realistic gain of slightly above $2 million. Ability to gain competitive advantage when disruption occurs.

Conclusion

This chapter has provided you with a road map for moving forward. This process is evolving today, and it relies on the ability of leaders to embrace the new thinking of the uncertainty advantage and to reconcile that thinking with managers and the markets. Whether you adopt the UTA or not, all actors (markets, leaders, and managers) have a common purpose: to solve problems and create permanent growth. To summarize, it requiring a reconciliation of the market, leader and manager mindset; laser focus on the situation and all of the elements of the UTA; and relentless pursuit of uncertainty.

Once the market driven strategy is selected and the UTA processes incorporated as part of the growth leader strategy then you are ready for the fire principles of execution. These principles are derived from this advanced process, and examined in detail in coming chapters. These principles accelerate the transformation. Getting these focused correctly is key to making the uncertainty advantage work. Without them, the process would fail.

These are

1. "Chapter 4: Focus—The Quest for Market Advantage Should Keep You up at Night"
2. "Chapter 5: Navigation—Manage Risk; Navigate Uncertainty"
3. "Chapter 6: Urgency—Markets Move Fast, but Organizations Do Not"
4. "Chapter 7: Details—The Devil Is in the Details, and This Requires Relentless Pursuit"
5. "Chapter 8: Priority—Growth Trumps Risk"

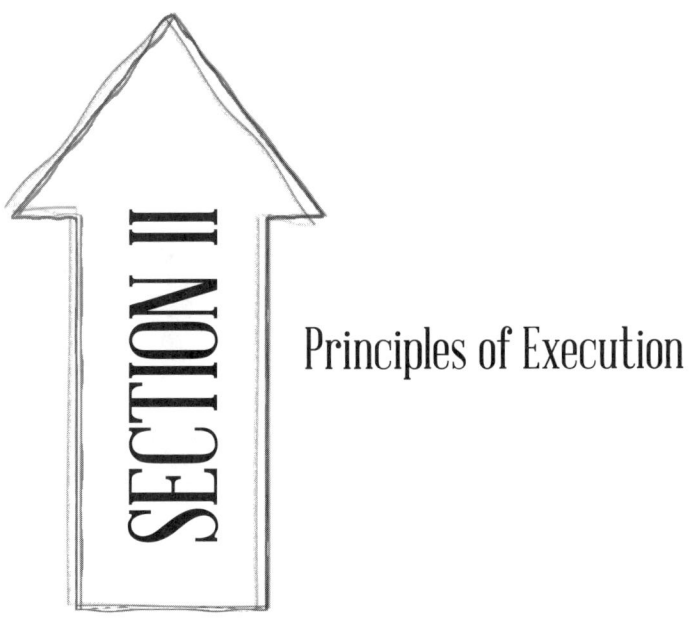

SECTION II
Principles of Execution

The key objective to growth and gaining market advantage is the tactical execution of the strategy. Understanding uncertainty better than anyone else and then navigating it to achieve market advantage requires a practical, realistic, and executable strategy. As Howard Shultz stated in his book, "Growth, we know all too well, is not a strategy. It's a tactic."[27] This points to the individual and the proactive mind-set. You navigate personally rather than managing what you can't influence; you move toward market-driven thought processes in a growth led system. This section demonstrates how uncertainty works and provides real-life examples and cases of how growth leaders improved decision-making and created market opportunity by maximizing uncertainty. This section also incorporates value creation and its principles, theories, and observations. Five principles (focus, navigation, urgency, priorities, and detail) are presented to serve as the foundation for adopting the uncertainty advantage mind-set as well as a road map or basis for putting this mind-set into action. The case histories and examples in this section demonstrate how other growth leaders have embraced uncertainty as a positive force for change.

---

[27] Howard Schultz, "Onward: How Starbucks Fought for Its Life without Losing Its Soul," Howard Schultz and Joanne Gordon, Rodale, March 27, 2012.

Focus: The Quest for Market Advantage Should Keep You up at Night

True growth leaders measure themselves on their abilities to create sustainable value in the market. Value is not defined from within but by the market—customers, investors, competitors, strategic partners, new entrants, regulators, and governments. Successful execution of this strategy requires impeccable and optimal performance, hence the primary focus, responsibility and reward system of the manager. But in the absence of the leader, stepping up to the pursuit of the uncertainty opportunity, the task is left to the managers. The priority quickly becomes either a compliance-, threat-, or performance-based strategy to managing risk. In other words, playing defense and measuring the best of the worst scenarios. But leaders are the ones closest to growth and with most at stake. They need to tap into the managers' competencies and capabilities by reconciling mindsets, providing incentives, applying a situational context, and leveraging data. The opportunity now exists for management to become part of the market facing growth process.

The quest for market advantage should keep you up at night. In this sense, the leader's uncertainty mind-set focuses on future impact and opportunity rather than past performance, financial engineering and failure to check the box.

When Change Is Imposed on You, the Importance of Color Choice Is Greater than You Think

Hyundai was effective in creating market advantage during a globally disruptive and imposed change, the disastrous 2011 earthquake and tsunami in Japan. The event shut down the only source for Xirallic, a pigment used on autos. It was produced in a single factory in Japan, a factory that was shut down after the March 11 earthquake. John Krafcik described this as "a case of a strong leadership team insisting on a solution that would keep all of the plants running."

In this case, a supply chain problem created a challenge and an opportunity. By once again applying the mind-set for understanding the uncertainty advantage and possessing the competencies and capabilities, Hyundai took on the problem and converted it to a competitive opportunity. Because other auto companies did not take on the problem with this mind-set, Hyundai created a clear market advantage. The focus was simple, relevant and relentless.

Xirallic, a paint pigment that made it sparkle, was used by all of the major auto manufacturers and it was produced by Merck KGaA, a single source operating from a single site in Onahama plant in Japan quake zone.[28] Hyundai management understood the uncertainty at both the organization and industry level. They also understood, and were prepared to react aggressively, that industry reliance on a sole source creates a market displacement opportunity. When the factory was closed for two months, the other auto manufacturers simply decided to stop using the pigment. Hyundai viewed this as an opportunity while others were mesmerized by the questions of "when" and "if".

---

[28] Hans Greimel, *"Pigment Maker's Lessons from Japan Quake"*, Automotive News, July 15, 2013.

Within five weeks, the company had overcome the problem by finding a new supplier and changing ingredients in its auto paints. The rest of the industry struggled with shortages through September, when Merck finally resumed full production.[29]

Krafcik says, "Our risk assessment asked whether replacement materials were close enough so that we could call it the same color. In most cases, we found the answer was no." An alternative had to be found and provided to numerous suppliers who painted various trim parts and delivered them to assembly plants. They listened, sensed, uncovered, and then pounced on the opportunity to channel uncertainty into a distinct market advantage.

"We were changing dozens of colors," Krafcik continued. "No other company was willing to tackle this issue. So for the Sonata model, we had one color for the first half of the model year and another color for the second half. We couldn't let the complexity prevent us from addressing the marketplace."

Other auto manufacturers restricted orders for vehicles in certain shades due to the unexpected shortage. That is a more common reaction to any shortage. Hyundai was able to create a clear market advantage by seeking alternatives, and in the process, eliminated the risk of relying on a single supplier.[30] "We were wired for the uncertainty opportunity," John concluded. The differentiator here was complex but clear. Rather than giving up on the problem, Hyundai figured out how to turn it into an advantage. The uncertainty itself created the opportunity, and this outside-the-box thinking defined how and why Hyundai was "wired," in Krafcik's words, to move forward boldly and with confidence.

The Uncertainty Advantage mind-set is critical for leaders but so too for managers and must be linked to their deep capabilities and competencies. These are best provided by internal and external subject matter experts. The next case highlights the importance of the linkage

---

[29] Chester Dawson, *"Quake Still Rattles Suppliers"*, Wall Street Journal, September 29, 2011.

[30] Deepa Seetharaman and Alina Selyukh, "Hyundai Finds Solution for Pigment Shortage," *Business News*, April 20, 2011.

through a CEO and industry growth leader point of view. It also provides an example of a change that was initiated rather than imposed.

Market Advantage: The Need for Competencies and Capabilities

I was returning home to the States on a flight from Stuttgart, Germany and, just by luck, happened to be seated next to Dr. Peter Leibinger, Vice Chairman of the Managing Board of the TRUMPF GmbH + Co. KG, head of the Laser Technology and Electronics division. Educated in mechanical engineering, Leibinger is part of a dynamic, diversified, leading company in industrial applications of laser technology. The company is also a world leader in sheet metal fabrication machinery.

Peter struck up a conversation, and as it always happens, the question came up, "What do you do?" He was very modest and did not disclose that he was an executive of a major organization. He shifted the conversation to focus on what I did (a dangerous question to ask a Management Consultant!). I responded with a story about how I help organizations navigate risk and uncertainty to their businesses. At the time, I had just released my second book, *Single Point of Failure: The Ten Essential Laws of Supply Chain Risk Management*. As a consultant, you learn to always have your business cards in your pocket, and in this case, of course, an extra copy of the book.

Peter was polite and tolerated my enthusiasm as I discussed the infamous Nokia, Ericsson, Philips case (yes, I describe it in this book as well; see chapter 6). To date, perhaps the best example of imposed change (a fire in a manufacturing plant) that allowed an aggressive and aware Nokia to capture significant market share over their primary competitor at the time, Ericsson. The uncertainty advantage, a market-driven reaction to change at its best.

Peter immediately internalized the story. His reaction was, "This directly applies to me, and this could have happened in our industry." Although his business was built around lasers and precision machines, he rationalized that the heart and soul (and possibly the biggest differentiator not of financial outcome but rather market advantage) was the production of the laser diode that went into precision cutting and punching machines used in the automotive, aerospace, furniture, and agriculture industries. It represented a small portion of the cost and revenue of the machine, but it defined perhaps the greatest single point of failure. Sales of machines were in the billions, but without the laser diode, they were useless. But even that revenue did not matter, since TRUMPF operated in a demanding and competitive market. It was about their future and their customers' futures. It was about positioning and responsibility. Financial impact mattered less in comparison to their reputation and stakeholder confidence. But loss of quality or unavailability of product translated into lost opportunity and, therefore, customer, investor, employee, supplier, and collaborator confidence. This all adds up to loss of market position and not doing what's in their best interest.

The discussion was enlightening and confirmed everything I was working on at the time. Several weeks later, Peter contracted for an extensive study to determine how well the organization was positioned and the degree of its vulnerability and readiness. Bottom line, he wanted to better understand uncertainty and needed help in getting focused on the topic of the risk and uncertainty of disruptive change (and I'm happy to report that as of the publication of the book he has continued to drive this mind-set across the organization).

As CEO Peter Liebinger, explained,

> You don't know what you don't know, and therefore, expert advice is necessary in some cases. A very good example for me was the fire hazard. I learned the majority of fires are caused by electricity. And poorly educated electricians that are working at your facilities are a danger. Our level of confidence and belief is naïve. To help people look in the right places, clearly it is an opening for someone to help others improve their business, even if businesses are very well run. However, the general theory is not enough unless it is derived from

use cases; i.e., what are general patterns and what must be looked at and how can they be found?

One aspect of growth is navigation of uncertainty, requiring knowledge and attention of where those vulnerabilities are most severe. This requires a 360-degree view, from market, leader, and manager perspectives. It also requires that you understand the expectation of the market and most important, competitors and potential new entrants; for this might be the uncertainty opportunity! This requires an assessment of displacement exposure, that is, barriers to entry or switching, the willingness for the market to switch, and the tipping point or factors where the switch or displacement becomes an obvious choice. At a minimum, what I witnessed in extreme cases of disruption and replenishment delays is an immediate shift in strategy to diversify the supply or demand base. In fact, the uncertainties inherent in exposures define how performance is best controlled and navigated. This requires analysis of products and services.

As the president of TRUMPF explained,

> The concept of uncertainty advantage has two aspects to it. First, it enables you to safeguard against risks with a different approach rather than setting up redundant operations. Second, if disaster strikes, I can move quicker and have an advantage. In both cases, with no disaster or with a disaster I have advantage.[31]

The TRUMPF experience is an excellent example of how deep insight, data and awareness to vulnerabilities can be converted into market advantage, and how a growth leader uses keenly focused risk processes and engages managers to make and prioritize investment decisions.

---

[31] Peter Liebinger, CEO, TRUMPF.

Turning Disaster into Opportunity: A Matter of Keen Focus

Not every change can be handled like the Hyundai or TRUMPF situations. In some cases, a big disaster points the way to great market advantage. For example, in the case of Vision-Ease, a catastrophic loss presented a clear uncertainty advantage.

Doug Hepper, executive chairman and former CEO of Vision-Ease Lens (VEL) had to act quickly in 2009 when faced with a major imposed change to the business; a disaster. Vision-Ease Lens, a leading supplier of optical lenses and among the first to develop and commercialize prescription polycarbonate lenses, had a history of navigating change and staying focused on the customer since being founded in 1930.[32] As the leader, Doug needed to look beyond the immediate consequences of the disaster. The company's Jakarta, Indonesia, factory burned down. How was this a market advantage opportunity? As Hepper explained, "It gave us an opportunity to build a state-of-the-art factory there in 2010." Doug summed up his philosophy as follows.

> "How you react, manage risk and resiliency is all built on a foundation. It is a reaction. Our foundation has always been taking care of the customer. The customer focus is always the starting point. Because of that, it drives you to behaviors that are different from that if you were just taking a financial view."

The disaster wiped out more than half of VEL's production overnight. They got through the experience quickly, by combining fast action, exceptional communication, and exceptional services to customers. It took seventeen months before full production was resumed. But turning loss into opportunity, VEL replaced and updated manufacturing equipment and held jobs for five hundred employees who

---

[32] http://www.insightequity.com/2014/09/30/insight-equity-announces-the-sale-of-vision-ease-lens/.

worked there before the fire.[33] By retaining its competencies, corporate memory, and knowledge, the Jakarta employees were able to rebuild a world-class facility.

VEL moved forward aggressively, put the customer and the market at the center, focused on returning to full production, absorbing the costs and improving their equipment. Too often, organizations seek ways to reduce costs at such times, to reduce the financial impact of a loss. This is exactly the wrong mind-set, one that ignores the market and the longer-term opportunity.

So VEL learned several critical lessons about the need for focus to turn disaster into market advantage.

- Crisis can be turned into opportunity; this is the differentiator.
- The leader, in this case Doug, is the credibility of the organization. Despite the chaos that initially ensues after a disaster like this, staying focused on the customer and market is paramount.
- Teamwork counts both for recovery and smart decisions for improvements.
- By caring, retaining, and absorbing the cost of the employees, you preserve the competency, corporate memory, and knowledge that provide an opportunity to rebuild something better.

Hepper explained, "The last measures we would look at are financial metrics ... they are a result of everything you do." Doug summed up his view of the uncertainty advantage: "In our industry you win business two ways, bids and when someone who has business lets the customer down [the one we prefer]." The market view matters most.

---

[33] "Vision-Ease Lens Resumes Full Production Following Fire at Indonesian Plant," *VM Magazine*, April 13, 2011; "Crisis: Lessons from Vision-Ease Lens," *The Optical Vision Site*, May 4, 2011.

> Do you believe in market advantage? The value of this assessment answers the question. If you are stuck in the outmoded thinking of margins above all else, you might be heading in the same direction as NBC in 2010. A comparison between Alan Horn of Warner Brothers and the NBC collaboration between Jeff Zucker and Ben Silverman makes this point and demonstrates why leadership mind-sets matter so much. The story was told by Anita Elberse, and it makes the point about belief in growth leadership. Alan Horn decided to go with a high-stakes strategy, picking four or five major investments out of twenty-five movies per year, and to focus all of their investment on these (including big-name stars, special effects, and marketing). The result was that for more than eleven straight years, Warner Brothers surpassed $1 billion in revenue. In comparison, Jeff Zucker headed up NBC, along with cochair Ben Silverman, in 2006. They chased after maximum margins, rather than ratings, as the priority. This was perhaps the biggest failure in entertainment history. The network moved to number four as the result of trying to cut costs and expenses. Zucker was asked to leave the company four years later, in 2010.[37]

The Hyundai and Roche cases from chapter 1 and the VEL and Hyundai Xirallic cases in this chapter were examples of imposed change. Similar to the Trumpf case, the experience at Starbucks provides insight into a initiated change by the growth leader. What followed was a focus on the market actors (and core values) and an incredible sense of urgency. The case also demonstrates the importance of careful navigation, supported by those with deep knowledge of uncertainty and an unbiased perspective; "it smells bad, it is bad".

---

[34] Anita Elberse, *Blockbusters: Hit Making, Risk Taking, and the Big Business of Entertainment* (New York: Henry Holt, 2013).

Starbucks—A Slow Brew

The Situation: Leader observed significant decline in strategic value, financial performance, and operational quality. Uncertainty about Starbucks as an ongoing, sustainable organization continued to escalate, it did so in an increasingly accelerating manner. The result was a deterioration of the store experience, unhappy employees, decrease in same store sales, and a 42 percent drop in the value of its stock.

The Change: Initiated by the CEO and ultimate growth leader. Observed, first hand, deteriorating store experience, deviating from heritage, not keeping pace with major technology trends, rapidly declining share price and same-store sales, and the infamous Schultz memo, "The Commodization of the Starbucks Experience."[35]

The Opportunity: Creating a transformation strategy and tactics to return Starbucks to its core values, establish an online and mobile experience, and reenergize leadership to support and execute the strategy. Navigate escalating uncertainty to sustain growth and market advantage.

Critical Business Decisions and Outcomes: Return to growth.

Manage the Financials or Navigate the Market-Focused Uncertainty Opportunity?

As CEO of Starbucks, Howard Schultz built an amazing empire based on a few subtle but essential ideas. Among these is the impression you get when you walk into a Starbucks. You literally can smell the coffee and feel the community spirit. This was the Starbucks market advantage and brand hook. Consistency and predictability were dominant attributes.

Schultz stepped aside as CEO to become what he described as a Bill Gates–style hands-off chairman. But it wasn't all that simple. By

---

[35] http://starbucksgossip.typepad.com/_/2007/02/starbucks_chair_2.html.

the summer of 2007, Starbucks was having its worst year ever based on declining profits and stock prices. Store traffic was down. Schultz concluded the company had spread itself thin by chasing expansion, opening too many stores too quickly. Uncertainty was percolating on all levels – the store experience, disgruntled and unengaging employees and financial performance that was far less than what the market expected. That year, Starbucks stock lost 42 percent of its value. The 2007 stock chart, shown in Figure 1.4, tells the story.

Illustration 9: The Transformation of Starbucks

For example, Schultz visited one of the company stores and was immediately struck by a pervasive odor: burned cheese. Gone was the appealing aroma of roasted coffee. It changed the entire atmosphere that had distinguished Starbucks from all other coffee shops. Shultz stated in his book, *"Onward"*,

> One day I walked into a Seattle Starbucks and immediately felt frustrated because burnt cheese had ... enveloped the store ... I left the store depressed. What would be next? Hash browns? The breakfast sandwich

became my quintessential example of how we were losing our way.[36]

He immediately ordered removal of sandwiches from all stores even though they represented a growing and profitable business. However, the new CEO heard of the mandate and countered it. Schultz fired the CEO and took that role back for himself, confident his opinion was correct and that the change was devastating and had to be remedied.

For Schultz, the last straw was not the financial trends but the smell of burned cheese and the uncomfortable feeling in his gut about the consequences of *rapidly accelerating uncertainty*.

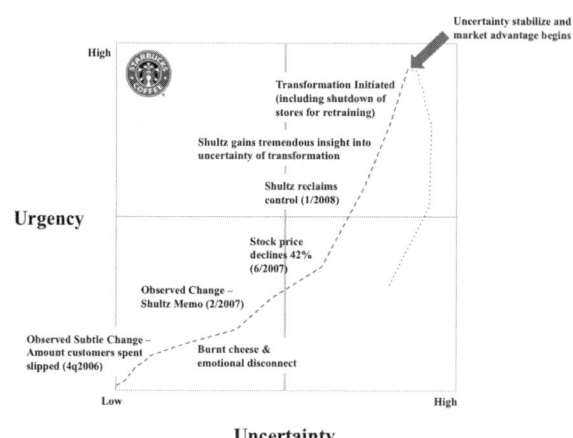

Illustration 10: Starbucks Urgency versus Uncertainty

You can look at this issue in one of two ways, especially when defining the leadership mentality involved. One way is to see this as a conflict between two leaders whose mind-sets could not be reconciled. This certainly is a problem, and determining the most beneficial outcome is complicated when two strong leaders will not budge and represent different biases regarding uncertainty. But the second way of

---

[36] Howard Schultz, *Onward: How Starbucks Fought for Its Life without Losing Its Soul* (Emmaus PA: Rodale Press, 2011), p. 37.

looking at this issue may clarify the conflict. Schultz was the true leader because his visionary mind-set went back to the original philosophy of Starbucks. He recognized that the company had moved away from a market rather than financial driven philosophy. In comparison, the new CEO, in countering Schultz's order to remove the cheese, may have failed to remember the original theme, driven not only by the investor but also by the customer. This meant one thing: he had failed to understand and pursue the escalating uncertainty at the store level and instead implemented a business strategy motivated by power and the numbers, not by what was right for the organization.

The question was how to revive the community spirit and the commitment to consistency. As a result, Schultz decided to reclaim the role of CEO. In January 2008, he took over once again as CEO and chairman.

Schultz was faced with two levels of imposed uncertainty. First was the uncertainty of what changes had occurred and why as well as a clear understanding of the market's interpretation. Second was the uncertainty about what his solutions would involve. His navigation skills would now have to compliment thorough management of the situation. After the coffee was burning with customers as well as employees. How could the reconciliation of the mind-set between managers and the market occur? What about the reconciliation of the leader (Howard Schultz) and the managers? At the time, all mind-sets were out of alignment:

- market and leaders (customer/store experience versus financial performance),
- leaders and managers (cookie cutter, loss of personal touch), and
- managers and the market (service to the customer, investor).

This is a story of a company's rapid growth, erosion, core values, and hubris caused by its own success. With a sense of urgency, Schultz navigated uncertainty closed down the entire Starbucks operation for a full day; a very expensive decision but necessary in his mind in order to retrain all employees in what really mattered. He concluded his philosophy: "Growth, we now know all too well, is not a strategy. It's a tactic."[37]

Schultz knew his own capabilities and demanded that the entire organization join with him in the same way. He is a perfect example of a thought leader whose philosophy viewed uncertainty as obstacles to achieving the business objectives and that leaders must continuously assess uncertainty and biases in their own behaviors. That's market navigation. He believed that if we make a mistake, we come clean about it and fix it immediately; we put your capabilities to work. Closing down the entire operation for a full day on February 26, 2008 was a bold and expensive move, and would no doubt bring Schultz a lot of criticism. But he didn't care about the financial loss or about the criticism. He had a vision, and it was the most important priority, far more important than profits. Knowing that he needed to recapture a deteriorating market advantage, his action was the most important thing. Profit equations did not enter the picture at all. So for three hours, 135,000 employees at 7,100 stores were retrained at an estimated cost of $6 million.

Rapidly escalating uncertainty and leadership inconsistencies were killing the enterprise. Schultz gained greater insight into uncertainty and then leveraged his competencies, combined with his internal resources, to identify and fix an urgent problem. For the first time in company history, Schultz looked to outside consultants for ideas on how to revive the company, and he had to do it quickly!

The emphasis among shareholders (the market) is always assumed to be on profits, dividends, and stock prices. In many cases, this is true. However, a more visionary outlook recognizes that profits do not matter in the immediate moment. Reorganizations would not solve the Starbucks issue. Profits are not the objective but the result of visionary leadership and a thorough understanding of the uncertainty that tomorrow brings (or at least consideration of it). It makes me wonder how shareholders would react to a chairperson of the board who did not pander to the desire for ever higher profits, bigger dividends, and

---

[37] Anne Fisher, "How Starbucks Got Its Groove Back," *Fortune*. March 24, 2012.

bigger market share but, instead, pointed to the vision for a permanently strong future. Profits, of course, would result, but they would no longer be the emphasis. The quest for market advantage should keep you up at night.

Would *your* chairman in that situation be applauded or replaced?

Schultz confronted serious uncertainty that demanded immediate actions. Would Starbucks survive? Was he acting in time? With declining stock prices and weakening financial results from overly rapid expansion, had the company peaked? Was it losing market advantage, and had it lost that advantage permanently? Would there be a mass exodus of carefully selected highly trained professionals? The only course left to him was to change direction, remind everyone of what made Starbucks different from all the ordinary coffee shop outlets, and resolve uncertainty.

The collective reasons for the success of Starbucks were a mystery to most people. But Schultz knew the reason for the company's success; the intangible collective mood and environment were expressed in the aroma of coffee and the atmosphere itself. This is what brought people in, kept them there, and insulated the company from any price resistance.

This is not only a case of transformation but also an example of the market over financials, strategy and uncertainty navigation and tactical execution at its best. For many, risk management has always been an operational and financial issue, a set of strategies to defensively respond to discovered losses or threats. In the case of Starbucks, the vision Schultz brought to the table had nothing to do with profit and loss in the immediate year but in returning to the concept of brand, not a measurement of risk or profitability, but an identification of potential market advantage.

The case raises an important question, however. Was Schultz truly exploiting uncertainty? Or was he simply practicing sound leadership and execution? In this situation, some traditional value preservation solutions might have occurred to management, including cutting back on the assumption that growth had occurred too rapidly, cutting costs and expenses in other ways, and raising prices. But these value preservation ideas would have ignored the intrinsic problem: the fact that the brand (the aroma of coffee) was lost temporarily.

Schultz recognized that the deterioration in the Starbucks brand presented a level of uncertainty that could be transformed into market advantage. This was not just another coffee shop but a one-of-a-kind welcoming environment. By taking back his leadership role, closing down for a day, and reorienting the staff, Schultz reiterated the core definition of the company and brought it back from the decline—not only by getting rid of the burned cheese odor but by defining once again what set the company apart from its competitors. Did he know it would work? Not necessarily, but he knew that taking no action would be sure to lead to failure. This, in a nutshell, is the uncertainty advantage.

Uncertainty as the Disrupter, with Market Focus Driving Execution ("Cash for Clunkers")

Hyundai's management positioning to recognize market advantage was not limited to the program of an insurance safety net discussed in chapter 1. The market-driven mind-set was deeply ingrained in the culture. During the recession, the government came up with the so-called "cash for clunkers" program. This program encouraged consumers to trade in their gas-guzzlers for higher fuel efficiency cars, including payment of a few thousand dollars regardless of trade-in value. Hyundai had noted that scrappage programs like this had been put into place in Germany even before the US program was designed. Krafcik said, "In late June, the CARS [car allowance rebate system] program was scheduled to start in July. But the details had not been announced and were estimated to be out by the end of July." Other auto companies took a wait and see attitude, but Hyundai, "took a very bold approach to embrace this uncertainty," according to Krafcik. "We said this program is coming for sure." This was the business change, and the execution of the CARS program represented the situation. The uncertainty differentiator in this case turned out to be the speed of execution. Hyundai leveraged their competence, through knowledge of the German scrappage program, and competencies to get in front of the market. In fact, they didn't know for sure, but their capabilities and intuition told them to go ahead and put the program in place.

According to Krafcik, "We were the first to offer this program, beating others by three weeks. We gave $4,000 to the dealer to give to the customer; there was uncertainty about the specifics of the program. Was there a potential downside? Sure. But we took action and made the program work." Three weeks ahead of their competition they understood uncertainty, focused on the market opportunity at the expense of potential financial exposure, and, as a result, set an all-time sales record for July and August. Hyundai sold out its inventory.

Hyundai performed an analysis to better assess and understand uncertainty. They understood their exposure and then made an intelligent and informed decision. This process is similar to that uncovered in the movie *21*, a true story of a professor who recruited college students to play out a system for winning blackjack in Las Vegas casinos.

This system involved a primary player, a secondary, and a signal person. These teams were able to take big money out of the casinos without cheating or breaking the law. There was a growth leader, a value enabler, and a team involved. The analogy between Hyundai's exploitation of market advantage and the blackjack story demonstrates the steps needed to create this in every organization.

1. Sensors: Listening posts, monitors, and a probing mind-set to quickly detect and or validate a change. These capabilities and competencies must be deployed at all levels of management and leadership as well as between market participants, such as strategic business partners. This is especially true of the front lines or deep in the operations of the business. There also must be a channel for moving the intelligence freely up and down and down and up the organization.

2. Analysis: Where do you get the data from, and what do you know from the data? The professor recognized the opportunity

to make money with a team approach to blackjack based on counting cards and spotting the trends. Hyundai knew that customers weren't buying cars due to concerns about job security.

3. Urgency: The immediate recognition of what we know about uncertainty provides a distinct advantage. Leader and managers must detect change quickly and then filter and escalate the observations in the context of the situation and market advantage. Critical to the process is the ability to quickly determine whether the situation contains the markers to invest in the pursuit of market advantage.

4. Degree of belief: The ability to quickly and with an unbiased mind-set reconcile the varying levels of confidence in the original assertions/hypothesis.

5. Execution: While staying focused on market advantage as the priority, leverage the managers' competencies and capabilities to provide timely, accurate, creative, and relevant input to the business decision. This includes going after the data. What are the available facts, and what problems and opportunities exist? Just as the gambling team had to understand the odds and trends in blackjack, a business has to know its customers' expectations. Also, explore inferences. What actions are drawn from the analysis? The blackjack team, working together, was able to develop a math-based working system to win. Hyundai saw that putting the assurance in place overcame customer concerns by promising them a way out if they lost their jobs.

Putting the program in place was a huge success and demonstrated that when market advantage is possible, you have to act quickly. Krafcik summarized, "We absolutely crushed it. We set an all-time sales record in July and again in August. We sold out our entire inventory. We had no cars left by the time the program was over. We succeeded in this because we had a bias to action; we appreciated the urgency of needing to do something. Benefits accrue to leadership. This played to our strengths."

The Strategy Risk Tipping Point: The Whirlpool Case

The great success enjoyed by Hyundai was due to an overriding awareness of markets and knowing how to exploit uncertainty. This recurring theme was obvious in all three examples: Hyundai Assurance to offset customer fears of job loss, fast action in the case of Cash for Clunkers, and aggressive market solutions to replace the loss of Xirallic.

The attributes at Hyundai were inclusion of strong and supportive managers under an effective growth leader and the willingness to listen to the value enablers on the team. So the capabilities, competencies, and behaviors at Hyundai worked together to exploit uncertainty and to create clear market advantage.

The VEL example contained a similar level of focus on market advantage, even given the different circumstances. A total disaster enabled the company to start over in a sense, exploiting the uncertainty of a sudden and unexpected loss into an improved situation. This loss, a situational opportunity, was used to turn events into a positive outcome. However, that was not the result in our Whirlpool example, a case of different kind of focus (and refocus). The company learned a tough lesson by focusing on cost reduction rather than on market advantage. The critical question was whether they adequately understood and reconciled the market, leader, and manager biases?

On the opposite side of the matter, if an organization's focus is strictly financial and ignores market advantage through quality and customer demand issues, the message gets lost. It makes sense to cut costs, but only if that is not done at the expense of market advantage. Whirlpool is a good case in point.

Whirlpool Case

In 2013, Whirlpool saw that it could save seventy-five cents per unit by outsourcing dishwasher water seals, projecting an annual savings of $2 million. But the manufacturer changed to a different rubber supplier, causing failure in 10 percent of units, meaning two million dishwashers had leaky seals. The cost to replace these was only part of the problem; the company's reputation suffered as well.[38]

If Whirlpool had approached this issue from a strategy risk and marketing point of view, they would have revisited their core customer beliefs and market differentiator, asked questions about quality, and assessed the uncertainty with an entirely different mind-set. This is a lesson worth learning; never assume you know what the market expects of your organization without constantly revisiting and revalidating the 360-degree market view (all market forces—customer, investor, competitor, regulator, strategic partners, government, special interests).

Capabilities, Competencies, and Mind-Sets: Questions Every Growth Leader Should Ask

Whirlpool was a case of putting focus in the wrong place. By focusing on the market instead of the bottom line, the problem could have been averted. But lesson learned. Markets matter more than the bottom line.

One attribute of effective growth leadership is found in the ability to look beyond the fundamentals of a uncertainty, to adopt the investor's point of view, and to appreciate how stakeholders view uncertainty and how to respond to it.

Key questions every growth leader needs to ask concerning uncertainty and the challenges that are associated with focus include several aspects. In seeking to create expansion into new markets, is our focus too heavily on financial issues? Or are we able to look beyond and understand the strategy risks? This is one aspect to change that has to

---

[38] Anne Freedman, "Meshing Distinct Viewpoints," *Risk and Insurance Magazine*, June 1, 2015.

be anticipated on the levels of regulatory uncertainties as well as markets. As with every example of change, the tipping points are critical and serve as inflection points, demanding great care when moving into action. At this point, a focus on decisions will determine whether focus is correct. For example, in the case of Hyundai, the question of how to move operationally never came up. The company focused on the customer.

At this point, leaders also ask themselves whether further improvements are required. How can we improve our core capabilities, competencies, and mind-sets to better identify and act on uncertainty? How will this lead to market advantage? And how do these definitions influence our decisions? This raises another issue; are our leadership styles defense or offense? In the case of Cash for Clunkers, most auto companies waited until the government finalized its rules, a defense mode. But Hyundai saw this uncertainty as a chance to get a jump on the opportunity, which converts over to offense. This was not a reckless move but a well-articulated and properly focused growth decision.

The key signals and indicators also have to be understood in this process. This is necessary in order for leaders to encourage value enablers not only to perform but to encourage their participation. And this requires measurement of market advantage itself. During this process, anomalies arise and have to be dealt with immediately. Finally, leaders cannot ignore the role of operations and finance as aspects of the uncertainty mind-set.

An analysis of the attributes exhibited by the preceding cases reveals many of the traits all growth leaders will want to follow. It often comes down to a fairly simple approach; when market facing, don't let operational and financial issues dominate your time, attention, and/or resources. Also, don't be limited by passive strategies, ones that measure what was and not what will be. Focus on developing capabilities, competencies, and mind-sets that create market advantages. The benefits to operational and financial interests will follow and fall into place.

Too much focus on operational and financial challenges or outcomes can also turn and bite you, even if it's only in the mind of the market and not the reality of the situation. Be keenly aware of how the market measures success or failure. For the customer it might be sentiment, confidence, trust; for competitors, it might be positioning; and for investors it might be forecasts, confidence, and future guidance rather than past financial results. For example,

> It was Tuesday, 21 Jul 2015 at 5:10 PM ET when Apple CEO Tim Cook said the company had an "amazing quarter." Unfortunately for him, investors care much more about the forecast. The iPhone maker predicted fiscal fourth-quarter revenue of $49 billion to $51 billion, trailing the $51.1 billion average analyst estimate in a Thomson Reuters survey. The company had little margin for error after a 39 percent jump in the stock price over the past year. Apple shares dropped 7.3 percent in after-hours trading.[39]

---

[39] http://www.cnbc.com/2015/07/21/apples-real-earnings-problem-the-forecast.html.

Navigation: Manage Risk, Navigate Uncertainty

Before the big game, athletes take to the field, practice their basic skills, and review the game plan one last time, always staying focused on the goal—to win. Once the game begins, they navigate obstacles and adapt, always relying on their basic skills, the game plan, and the ultimate goal. They cannot control the crowd, the opposing team's strategy, the way the referees officiate the game, the condition of the playing surface, or a dozen other factors—each of which can influence the outcome. This is the essence of navigating uncertainty as it applies to business today. You operate in a market without borders no longer as a stand-alone, insular entity but as a boundary-free network of relationships with common interests. What unifies—the goal—is the ability to collectively deliver value to the market while creating value for stakeholders and yourself. You navigate business across industries, geographies, and partnerships, always staying focused on your goal. Each change presents opportunity and uncertainty. Not all change is equal. To stay nimble, flexible, and adaptable, you need basic skills (mind-set, competencies, and capabilities), a game plan, and clear business goals. It's a journey, change by change, situation by situation. You arm yourself with mastery of three pervasive segments of uncertainty navigation: (1) probing and sensing; (2) filtering, dialogue, and decision; and (3) executing, adapting, and learning. This chapter lays out the navigational transformation now under way, one that is rapidly moving away from reactive, highly structured management toward the market-driven strategy of value creation.

The concept "growth leaders need to navigate uncertainty" as a prerequisite of capturing market advantage has been introduced in prior chapters. But what is meant by "navigation" and how does a growth leader go about executing this principle? Let's face it; executing the growth strategy requires the participation of diverse market, leaders, and managers' stakeholders and a reconciliation of their needs. All vary in size, markets, and geographies they serve and mind-sets defined by personal incentives. It's all about navigating change to support critical decision-making, ultimately to gain leverage in the market (not ownership). It's about how you establish it, the speed at which you can gain it, how you apply it, who's got it, and who can make the most with the least. Perhaps the greatest opportunity to gain leverage is when great uncertainty and change are anticipated or become reality. That is when the uncertainty transformation agenda (UTA) and uncertainty advantage mind-set, capability, and competencies pay off and navigation begins. Unlike risk management of the change, the initial goal is not to apply rules or calculate the probability of an adverse event or the return on a risk investment. The goal is to identify change, understand uncertainty, uncover opportunity, and enhance the original business goals. Bindiya Vakil, CEO and founder of Resilinc Corporation, a supply chain risk intelligence and analytics solution provider, summed up navigation as follows.

> "The word manage does not have direction or a destination underlying it; to navigate means that I'm

heading towards a particular destination or outcome and continuously course correcting when the environment changes. If I'm not navigating but rather managing, in an uncertain environment, I might be drifting and at best, surviving. I can also manage myself into a bad situation, however, when I navigate, I always have the final destination in mind and I am constantly adjusting for intrinsic and external changes. Navigation presupposes access to tremendous amounts of intelligence. Navigation requires an advanced level of intelligence and insight. It also necessitates assessment of vulnerability and impact analytics that are predictive, so that priorities can be set for allocating scarce resources and budget. This is the essence of course correction. Navigation inherently includes continuous action. For one of our customers, intelligence driven supply chain navigation began as a "risk" initiative. Their challenge was they had capability but it was fragmented by diverse tools. It made it very difficult to centrally harness the competence and capability in an actionable manner.

Once the customer fully deployed an advanced intelligence and analytics supply chain resiliency solution, they quickly discovered that all their supply chain intelligence was at their fingertips. Now they could enable the leaders with tremendous insight into uncertainty. They were able to predict the most critical vulnerabilities and potential impact quickly so that they could detect and resolve problems before they escalated into major disruptions. In one year this client had to course correct and respond to more than 300 adverse supply chain risk events, 800 supplier part change notifications, 55 conflict minerals non-compliance incidents and about 20 Corporate Social Responsibility incidents.

The active scanning and early detection together with ready impact predictions helped them respond and recover and return to their target destination. In the process, they were able to minimize risk, but most importantly, they were able to leverage this capability to gain market advantage. The solution provided them with great, real-time insight into how a particular incident or change would impact their business. They used this intelligence to then act and replenish inventory quickly or absorb supply-driven pricing shocksà before their competition. Then when their competition was raising prices or struggling to meet customer demand, they were there signing long term contracts and challenging the market dynamic. Even getting to the decision that an incident had no impact was valuable because it led to greater efficiency and allocation of scarce resources while ensuring the organization did not drift. For me, the directional component is the essence of navigation".

In a *Harvard Business Review* article titled "Management Risk: A New Framework,"[40] the authors introduced a new categorization of risk that suggests executives choose between a rules-based model for preventable or internal risks, a strategy-risk model for major innovation and investments, or an external-risk model to manage risks created by external events. Setting aside for a moment the differences between managing and navigating, the point is that there are alternatives and, more important although not explicitly stated, there is need to navigate not manage strategy risk. These risks are not inherently undesirable, however, strategy with high expected returns generally requires the company to take on significant risks. Translation: they must thoroughly

---

[40] Robert S. Kaplan and Anette Mikes, "Management Risk: A New Framework," *Harvard Business Review*, June 2012.

understand and navigate uncertainty at a level that typically doesn't exist. By becoming proficient at it, you are able to uncover uncertainty advantage and market opportunity. How does an organization go about doing this? To do so requires a dialogue (competency), rather than dictation, for the given situation among managers and external experts with deep competencies and capabilities as well as an extensive understanding of behavioral, emotional, and cognitive biases that interfere with the ability to gain a clear, concise, and objective picture of the opportunity and uncertainty. The executive team will also need to price these out and incorporate them into the expected performance model.

Uncertainty Navigation - Probing and Sensing

Navigating for today doesn't matter ... as much. The executive team of a leader in the packaged goods and food industry, best known for agricultural commodities, became concerned with the potential for disruptive change caused by several growing social, economic, and environmental trends. At issue was the question of how a growing population in the future could be fed with existing resources. As the middle class was expanding and farmable land shrinking, other issues arose—volatile weather and increased weather events, water shortages, volatility in prices, and more exposure on the supply side. The Executive team recognized these issues could lead to structural change (UTA marker), not only from the supply chain point of view, but also as an issue for business leaders to consider.

They applied their leadership efforts to maximize their market-driven competency in looking to the future. This case led to a deeper understanding of what mattered most to the market, made up of farmers, regulators, governments, communities, and strategic business partners. It also led to development of a long-term view for the company's growth plans. But what it also led to was the development of a market-driven mind-set, one with deep competencies and capabilities that extended far beyond financial engineering. In an interview with the Director, Supply Chain Strategy, she shared the following wisdom regarding market advantage.

> You can see as a risk and manage when it happens or you can see at as a competitive advantage and do things more proactively—invest long term—From consumer perspective a bit harder to justify investment, however, halo effect if you go beyond financial engineering - engage consumer what's important and you can improve performance. Go back 10 years and it didn't make any sense to engage farmers backward engineering - a victim of supply chain de-verticialization.

This overall challenge in navigation was not merely a procurement problem for the manager but a bigger problem for the growth leader. The known risks were associated beyond the risk equation and potentially offered a competitive advantage through proactive navigation. The company knew it would need to make a long-term investment in creating this advantage. The debate centered on the need for a new, market-driven concept and culture. An awareness of the limitations growing from past efforts at de-verticalizing the supply chain. That was a defensive move, not driven by expanding markets.

Among the changes the organization pursued investing in farming, running pilot farms for some of the agricultural commodities they marketed (competencies and capabilities). They retained agronomists to identify methods for improving farm practices and crop yields (acquired/broadened competencies). This was part of a cultural effort to convert fear into advantage (mind-set).

Leadership was engaged at the level of discussions with farmers and not merely as executive oversight functions. This made all the difference in the organization's view. The culture was to transition away from reactive risk management to seeing risk as the generator of competitive advantage. To accomplish this goal, the Executive team needed to move away from the viewpoint of this as a procurement problem and supplier risk. They needed to invest in farming, engage across the entire supply chain, and recognize that farmers had choices. This was a market-driven mind-set and was enabled by aggressively probing, sensing, and understanding current and future uncertainty.

The organization further recognized that they had to move away from passive reliance on downstream suppliers (mind-set). The company's core competency was the key to differentiating the company in the marketplace. One conclusion of this change, according to the Director, was that "If we don't take more risk, someone else is going to do it." If this reminds you of Steve Jobs, Jeff Bezos or Amar Bose and their early recognition of the market, it should; it is the same idea.

Calling the program a "strategy piece," executive leadership recognized that risk management as a reactive science was not going to work in the future. The market had become competitive, not just in the well-understood sense, but in the sense of how the future has to be anticipated and maximized.

A related challenge was faced by Monsanto. Growth had traditionally been measured in terms of revenue, profitability, market development effectiveness, and market share. However, what was missing was a deeper view through the market lens (mind-set), including the uncertainty surrounding key issues such as grower satisfaction, grower loyalty, grower segmentation, signature touch point implementation, and measuring the progress of implementation.[41] A shift to market advantage required more emphasis on initiatives aimed at fixing this problem. With the high profile Monsanto had in the market (and not all positive) the brand issue was one of the keys. They too had realized that they did not control all aspects of the business and therefore manage away the issues. Instead they had to carefully navigate the market stakeholders. This was a revelation to Monsanto, whose belief in their product led to a set of inaccurate assumptions and intuitive beliefs.

---

[41] http://www.monsanto.com/sitecollectiondocuments/csr_reports/monsanto-pledgereport-2005.pdf.

Uncertainty Navigation - Filtering, Dialogue, Decision

Disruptive change sometimes is introduced without notice, resulting in unforeseen consequences. The entire hard disk drive (HDD) technology industry experienced disruptive change in the third and fourth quarters of 2011 as a result of massive flooding in Thailand. At the time, Thailand assembled about 40 percent of the world's hard drives, and if you account for drive component manufacturing, it's the global leader according to Fang Zhang, a storage analyst at market research firm IHS iSuppli. Navigation in cases of structural change and disruptions emphasizes the need to monitor, uncover trends or quickly identify events, understand the ramifications by deeply understanding interconnectivity and interdependencies, initiate a dialogue (there's no one way of doing things, even with a plan), and quickly make decisions. Filter, dialogue, and decision is the second phase of navigating uncertainty. This type of forward-looking thought process was enacted by Western Digital (WD) when the company realized it had a tough decision concerning the future of their business after a catastrophic disruption. Initially viewed as market and operations recovery, the effort provided market advantage by minimizing the impact on their market and organizational stakeholders, and by adjusting their operational model to provide greater resiliency going forward. Also considered was the possibility of a faster ramp-up and roll-out of an alternative technology, the solid state drive (SSD). The disaster affected many industries, notably auto manufacturing and technology industries, including WD, who, at the time of the event, manufactured and supplied one third of the world's supply of hard disk drives.

Three months after the disaster, John Coyne, WD president and CEO, said that Thailand needed, "a credible plan, well executed with measurable milestones along the way, and we need to define those milestones quickly."[42]

---

[42] Thomas Fuller, "An Industry Stalls in Thailand Amid Flood Debris," *New York Times*, January 21, 2012.

In a sense, controlling 40 percent of the world supply of any product could work against a growth leader. That's a comfortable competitive position, so it is all too easy to forget to recognize change, not to mention navigating the uncertainty of it. WD had to be able to filter its thought process to overlook its strong market position and focus on the uncertainty itself. Without doubt, a dialogue between managers and leaders began as a conflict of priorities. However, from their actions, it is clear that the growth leader's ideas prevailed, and the uncertainty advantage led the way. In fact, the following year, WD had recovered fully.

What had to be accomplished to remain focused on market advantage? No one can navigate everything at the same time. So among WD's decisions was emphasis on one of its three major lines of business, the OEM channel (outlets providing products to large scale original equipment manufacturers as well as corporate enterprises) while putting on hold two other major channels, direct distribution and retail markets. This is clearly an out-of-the-box form of thinking. How many managers would think about putting two-thirds of their channels on the back burner? The analysis of what truly were priorities led to this decision, and once analyzed, it became clear that it was the only sensible course of action.

This decision to focus on the OEM and Enterprise channels meant recovering flooded equipment used in the OEM lines as a first priority.

> A year after a flooding disaster in Thailand took out a large portion of hard disk production, the industry has fully recovered with shipments to the computer market expected to hit a record level this year.[43]

The most extensive flooding—and the primary focus of this report—occurred between late July and early December across nearly every section of the country. In total, sixty-five of Thailand's seventy-seven

---

[43] Lucas Mearian, "Disk Drive Shipments Rebound from Thai Floods," *Computerworld*, September 28, 2012.

provinces were impacted during this time frame, and damage was widespread and severe in many locations. Economic losses were estimated by the World Bank at THB1.4 trillion (USD45.7 billion), which makes the floods one of the top five costliest natural disaster events in modern history. The insurance industry, which plays a vital role in the risk management of various sectors, insured at least THB337.0 billion (USD10.8 billion) in losses (as published by Thailand's Office of Insurance Commission), and the industry has already undergone major changes as a result. Many insurers have started to seek a change in flood insurance policy coverage, modifying the current structure that sees flood insurance typically included with fire coverage.[44]

Major flooding in the monsoon season of October 2011 created the disaster. This was by no means an isolated threat; the monsoon season returns every year, so WD needed to take action to prevent future losses while regaining its market advantage. It was the reaction of WD to their specific threat as well as prioritizing its markets that helped the company recover within one year.

> Western Digital's hard-disk drive production in Thailand ground to a halt when nearly two-foot high floodwater washed through the 1.1 million square-foot facility ... Western Digital Corp., one of Thailand's largest foreign employers, moved some manufacturing of hard—disk drive components from Thailand to Malaysia ... [WD] has also moved key equipment to the second floor and is spending $20 million to build a 9-foot concrete wall around the company's 24-acre property ...[45]

The experience was revealing in the extent of loss as well as WD's fast recovery. It took a full week for the water to recede. WD had to

---

[44] "2011 Thailand Floods Event Recap, Report Impact Forecasting", AONBenfield, March 2012.

[45] Kathy Chu, "After Floods, Business Still Wary of Thailand," *Wall Street Journal*, October 5, 2012.

send in divers and cranes to pull equipment out of the headquarters. By the way, this also took place with the presence of snakes and alligators in the clean room.

In deciding which equipment to pull out first, WD decided to focus on equipment to get the OEM line up and operating as quickly as possible. With over one-third of all disk drives previously produced in the Thailand plant, WD was looking at a long lead time to rebuild if they tried to get all markets back into full operation. During recovery, they faced losses of $180 million in the first quarter and another $110 million in the following quarter. The market advantage was derived by working with the Thai government to improve diking in the entire district as well as the massive concrete walls built around the facilities.

It took forty-six days for the plant to come back online. The analysis of risk, cost of recovery, and lost efficiency had not been addressed prior to this incident. WD asked itself, "Is this what we want? How do we overcome the market challenge? What tools, methods, and models do we need to optimize resiliency while also optimizing efficiency?"

The company had operated in Thailand for twenty years, a long-term commitment to employment and industry for the country. To this day, the Thailand plant continues operations in full swing and is still WDs largest production site. Market advantage was gained by improving education and development of a skilled labor force. WD continued paying all of its employees during the downtime, and all employees returned to work.

WD made a decision to focus on market advantage in the OEM market and defer recovery efforts in the other two market lines. They were truly navigating the high waters. The solution was not to pace the dark hallways, imagining unaffordable losses. The solution was to strategically identify the strongest market for WD and to focus only on that market. The result was a reduced risk universe on the marketing side and a success story in the production end.

Navigating the High Seas

Cantor Fitzgerald analyst Laura Champine has noted, "Anything that disrupts retail is very good for the off-price guys."[46]

This was the clear message in the experience of port disruptions. Navigation and opportunity appliers, of course, not only to uncertainty on land, but just as much to uncertainty on the high seas. In 2015, global supply chain problems arose due to gridlock in West Coast ports.

This was caused largely by months of delay in a labor dispute. Cargo was shifted to the East Coast, Gulf Coast, western Mexican ports, and Canadian ports. To avoid congestion in US western ports, cargo was relocated and added congestion and transportation costs on land. By March 2015, two-thirds of shippers responded to a survey by saying they would ship less cargo through the western ports in the United States during 2016, and some announced permanent rerouting plans.[47]

The long-term strike in ports, where 50 percent of overseas goods normally offload, took a big chunk out of commerce in 2015. Maersk Line cancelled some sailings, and China Ocean Shipping announced plans to skip at least one port. Truckers accustomed to hauling up to five containers per day from the Port of Oakland hauled one per day at the most. The big effect is felt by small businesses and many others. On the export side, the cost was just as heavy. The Agriculture Transportation Coalition estimated that port congestion was costing $1.75 billion per month in agricultural exports.[48] All of this created massive structural and disruptive change.

Not everyone suffered from the port disruptions, however. The growth leaders of off-price retailers like TJX gained market advantage

---

[46] Ramkumay Iyer, "Off-Price Retailers Strike Gold from West Coast Slowdown," *Reuters*, May 19, 2015.

[47] Laura Stevens, "Ports Gridlock Reshapes the Supply Chain," *The Wall Street Journal*, March 5, 2015.

[48] Laura Stevens, Suzanne Kapner, and Leslie Josephs, "Port Delays Starting to Damage Businesses," *The Wall Street Journal*, February 16, 2015.

by exploiting the risk and snapping up orders canceled by traditional stores during the congestion following the labor dispute. "It created an opportunity for off-price retailers to capitalize on the plethora of merchandise available in the market place at very favorable prices," said Stifel analyst Richard Jaffe. TJX also raised its profit and sales forecasts, benefitting from bargain hunting shoppers.

What can growth leaders do to offset these losses and to navigate them to create market advantage? Smaller companies may be better equipped than larger ones to find alternatives to imports and navigate uncertainty (i.e., similar to the Hyundai example in chapter 1). Local sourcing or sourcing from Canada or Mexico, using trucking and rail delivery systems, are one way to navigate around the port bottlenecks. For exporters, shipping out of Canadian ports may be one alternative; if this is possible with favorable timing and pricing, the market advantage may be part of the solution. Larger concerns, like import-heavy Walmart, have a bigger problem. They do not keep long-term inventory available but rely on just-in-time delivery and minimal warehousing. This translates to empty shelves in stores for many of their products. However, larger companies may also need to rely on shorter supply chains and more local or nearby sources rather than on the massive Asian supply chain currently used by big concerns.

The entire question of navigation on many levels has to be addressed by growth leaders. The need to navigate uncertainty relates to post-disaster response and equally to pre-disaster planning, to brand improvement, to internal communications, and to work slowdown and strike incidents that may go on for the long term.

Cummins and the Heavy-Duty Truck Engine

The leaders at Cummins was able to exploit uncertainty through an initiated change to build market advantage over its much larger competitor, Caterpillar. In 2002, Caterpillar and the American Trucking Association (ATA) lobbied the EPA to reverse or even throw out planned 2004 emission standards for diesel-fueled trucks. The failure to escape the new restrictions led to Caterpillar leaving the heavy-duty truck engine market by 2010.

Uncertainty about whether emission standards would affect the industry or who would fill the void left by Caterpillar was settled when smaller competitor Cummins stepped in and took over the lion's share of this market. Having developed their XPI fuel system, Cummins figured out how to reduce emissions. In 2012, Cummins introduced its new ISX12 engine, combining improved fuel efficiency with lower maintenance costs and better performance. The market advantage Cummins gained was based on Caterpillar's inability to escape new emission standards and its decision to simply leave the market. Rather than navigating the complexity of compliance, Caterpillar navigated out the door.

At the same time, Cummins developed improved technology to meet standards and take over the US market for heavy truck engines. Where Caterpillar had once dominated the market, these changes allowed Cummins to move quickly and take over a majority of diesel engine sales for heavy trucks.[49]

This was a good example of how market advantage is created through understanding and navigation of strategy risk. Cummins would not have been able to compete head to head for this business until Caterpillar abandoned it. When strategy risk is the driving force, a company is able to succeed in building market advantage. However, if a company focuses on operations or finance, it is misguided and likely to make expensive mistakes. Navigation is the common element, whether dealing with the competition or with internal security. A comparative example follows.

---

[49] "Caterpillar and Truckers Fight to Step Clean-Up of Dirty Diesel Engines," National Resource Defense Council (NRDC), July 9, 2002; "Caterpillar Exits On-Highway Engine Business." *Today's Trucking,* June 13, 2008, www.todaystrucking.com; "Cummins Filtration to Support SCR Equipped 2010 Engines with Diesel Exhaust Fluid," *CumminsEngines.com,* January 8, 2009.

Uncertainty Navigation - Executing, Adapting and Learning

GM and Toyota: A Comparison of Auto Recalls

Is your focus in the right place? When management is allowed to use the question of profitability to *avoid* the market-driven path, it invariable fails. A case in point is a comparison between GM and Toyota in 2014.

GM recalled 29 million cars worldwide in 2014, following thirteen deaths and fifty-four crashes due to a faulty ignition switch. Chevrolet Cobalt models were the culprits. The way GM handled this is instructive in comparison to the Toyota response in 2009–2010 when acceleration problems led to recalls. In the case of Toyota, an attempt to diffuse the situation through public relations—including denial that the problem even existed—nearly destroyed the company.

The Toyota error was instructive to GM, and it reacted in a very different way. The GM focus was not on the profits impact but on markets. As a result, sales and profits rose after the recalls, when you would naturally expect them to fall. Why? Jessica Caldwell, senior analyst with Edmunds, explained, "You'd think it would damage their brand, but it's actually helping to drive purchases at the dealerships."

Recalls brought people into the dealerships, of course. But GM saw this as an opportunity and focused its energies there. In July 2014, GM posted its best monthly sales in seven years despite the massive round of recalls. They sold over 256,000 cars that month alone, a 9 percent uptick from one year before. The consumer visits to the dealership as part of the recall sparked more trade-in activity than would have occurred without the recall. GM offered attractive low-cost financing coupled with employee-level pricing, a 34 percent discount from retail price.

Market focus was the key. The first step in auto sales is always getting people to visit the dealership. The recall accomplished that. The captive audience was on hand for the time needed to replace the ignition switch. During this time, new models with upgraded features convinced customers the timing was good for a trade-in. This was further encouraged with the discounts and attractive financing.

Autodata Corp. reported that before the recall, GM owned 16.9 percent of the market; after the recalls, market share rose to 18.8 percent. This case, turning uncertainty into market advantage, was due to focus on smart sales, exploiting the situation to make GM stronger, not weaker.[50]

Focus is the key. A first instinct for organizations facing negative publicity is to go on defense. Toyota tried that, and it only made matters worse. GM saw the opportunity within the uncertainty of the recall. By navigating that uncertainty with smart sales tactics—having customers in the dealership, discounts, attractive financing—the company was able to create marketing success out of the recalls. Toyota took the defensive and reactive risk management approach, arguing that the problems customers had were not due to accidental acceleration. In other words, "You can't prove it was our fault," a terrible example of how to handle a problem. At one point, Toyota even speculated that the accidents were caused by the drivers. In comparison, GM focused on the uncertainty advantage and created a market opportunity.[51]

The GM case is instructive, especially in comparison to Toyota's reactive and profit-motivated response in a similar situation. With proper focus, GM presented a perfect model of how uncertainty can be converted in a positive manner. Focus on proactive decisions with situational strategies to exploit uncertainty to create market advantage.

The whole concept of navigation has to respect how leverage works. You cannot navigate everything, and in fact, you cannot own everything. You have direct control over very little. However, skillful navigation lets you act as growth leader and influence how others may function, even in the most complex set of uncertainties (risk) and doubts (opportunities). The use of leverage to lead is a function of how effectively you navigate uncertainty.

---

[50] Aaron M. Kessler, "G.M. Sales Rise as Buyers Ignore Recalls," *The New York Times*, July 1, 2014.

[51] Michele Wang, "Why Did GM Sales Increase after Recalls?" *Beyond.com*, July 26, 2014.

Navigation is not a simple matter. It has meanings on many subtle levels, which encompass both operational and financial risk management and focus on marketing strategies. The lessons of the cases in this chapter make this point, all in different ways.

The package goods and food industry organization had to contend with the realization that navigation is not just short term but has to be applied with an eye to the distant future. Monsanto was in a similar situation, but for it, navigation dealt more with its brand and reputation and the need to improve outreach. In the case of WD, the issue was immediate, and action had to be taken quickly to overcome the disaster. But it contained navigation on several levels.

The lack of growth leadership among HDD manufacturers both before and after their disaster in 2011 is a teaching moment for growth leaders everywhere. Has WD ever addressed its lack of planning, or has the company mitigated risk exposure and returned to business as usual? Does the company continue to live with vulnerabilities associated with its limited number of suppliers? What additional changes could it make to navigate uncertainty? And finally, does WD even believe it needs to undertake this initiative?

In the traditional mode of thinking, operations and financial managers think they have done all they need to do by responding to disaster by mitigating exposure (moving equipment, building dikes, etc.). But is this enough?

Growth leaders can learn as much by what is not being done by WD as they can by what was done in advance or in the moment when uncertainty arose in the three examples previously explained in the case of Hyundai.

Yet another navigation lesson was learned from the port disruptions. Navigation in this case involved not only the immediate problem but the need to evaluate the entire supply chain on a global basis to avoid problems of delays in the future. In this instance, navigation involved extremely time-sensitive navigation in the movement and off-loading of cargo

Cummins navigated a big problem in a much different manner. The EPA demands made on heavy truck emissions standards were so extreme that Caterpillar simply abandoned the business. Could Cummins turn that into market advantage? By navigating the emissions requirement challenges, it turned a market problem into market advantage. In comparison, the GM/Toyota example revealed another form of navigation: Two companies facing a similar issue responded in very different ways.

> Every growth leader can learn from the wisdom of Mario Andretti, who observed, If everything seems under control, you just not going fast enough.

6

Urgency: Markets Move Fast, but Organizations Do Not

Uncertainty is urgent without exception, which is exactly why you need to navigate your personal decisions and expectations. Three critical aspects of urgency are explained through case histories in this chapter. These are (1) markets move fast but organizations do not; (2) if you don't act quickly, your competitors will; and (3) the growth leader welcomes uncertainty as part of the opportunity for making informed decisions to deliver on expected outcomes.

The growth of the Internet, social networks, and mobile computing has allowed for ideas and information to flow more freely, broadly, and at an unprecedented rate. From a growth perspective, this has enabled new entrants into the markets and provided access from anywhere in world. This growth has also facilitated the integration of businesses, third parties, and supply chains. This dramatic change in operating models has also created enormous uncertainty and with it, opportunity. For an imposed change, such as the case of the hedge fund presented in chapter 2, the expanded listening, monitoring, filtering, and understanding uncertainty capabilities provided them with the opportunity to not only know more than the market but also allowed them to operate faster than the market. For a change initiated by the growth leader, speed at which they can execute their decisions becomes a significant market differentiator when possessing greater insight into uncertainty and, thus, a more concise, realistic, and unbiased strategy. In this chapter, we probe deeper into the urgency principle and analyze several cases where speed and timing were significant factors in gaining the uncertainty advantage.

Why Is the Uncertainty Opportunity Urgent?

Uncertainty is always urgent. So once a growth leader recognizes the opportunity growing out of uncertainty, history has shown that it does not last for long. Failure to act means the opportunity is lost. Because the first instinct during times of uncertainty is to stop and wait to see what happens next, many opportunities have been lost. In the Hyundai case, presented in chapter 1, growth leader John Krafcik recognized that the large/OEM auto manufacturers would not be able to move as fast as Hyundai. The ability to respond to the urgency was a key competency and market differentiator. The concept of "shared value" comes into play in this situation, as well, if you hope to create permanent and long-term market advantage.

In discussing a traditional approach, or a specific strategy designed around operational and financial priorities, management is likely to oversimplify the issues. As one author wrote,

> One danger is that this traditional approach leads executives to view uncertainty in a binary way – to assume that the world is either certain, and therefore open to precise predictions about the future, or uncertain, and therefore completely unpredictable. Planning or capital-budgeting processes that require point forecasts force managers to bury underlying uncertainties in

their cash flows. Such systems clearly push managers to underestimate uncertainty in order to make a compelling case for their strategy.[52]

This description, addressing uncertainty by reverting to the familiar even though it does not work, is one way that urgency can force poor decisions. However, there is an alternative. By navigating urgency in the same way that you navigate uncertainty, you can create a completely different reaction based on proactive, market-driven strategy. Ericcson, a supplier to Nokia, was one such case. Both organizations faced uncertainty, and responded with a sense of urgency.

Nokia and Ericcson: Solutions through Uncertainty

Market advantage may come from realizing what has to be done to create innovative growth with a futuristic vision. I call those who are able to accomplish this uncertainty visionaries. The difference between risk and uncertainty is in how far a reaction goes and on how urgently a growth leader acts. Old-style risk management was reactionary, a process of identifying losses after they occurred and then taking steps to prevent them in the future, or to identify known risks and mitigate them through insurance or changes in processes. The risk manager did little else. But the uncertainty visionary, the growth leader, goes a step farther, looking for ways that the loss could be turned into a market advantage with awareness that the opportunity does not wait but has to be acted upon with urgency.

An example of how this occurred was the case of Ericsson, a major supplier to Nokia. They had to confront an imposed change. As I explained in my last book,

> A well-recognized business case that shows the benefits (and consequences) of urgency and quick decision

---

[52] Hugh Courtney, Jane Kirkland, and Patrick, "Strategy under Uncertainty," *Harvard Business Review*, November 1997.

making with regard to uncertainty involves a major supplier to Nokia that produces semiconductors for Nokia phones. The company suffered a fire in a "clean" room at its plant in Albuquerque, New Mexico, on March 17, 2000. Smoke spread throughout the facility and contaminated wafers in almost every stage of production, destroying millions of chips in just a few minutes. Consequently, production of cell phone chips intended for Nokia and its competitor, Ericsson was halted. Nokia quickly realized that the disrupted supplies would prevent production of some four million handsets and could impact 5 percent of its annual production. The team quickly ascertained the availability of alternate sources for the parts. Nokia responded by working with existing suppliers to ensure that Nokia operations would continue with minimal interruption.

When it was clear that the much-needed chips were significantly delayed, lower-level employees at Ericsson did not communicate the news to their bosses (lack of urgency). The head of the consumer electronics division did not learn of the problem until several weeks after the fire. By the time Ericsson realized the magnitude of the problem, it was too late and it lost market share to Nokia. If Nokia were to follow the Band-Aid approach, it would have stopped after the disrupted supplier had recovered. However, it took further action following this event. Nokia developed a series of visibility systems to track major shipments of all of its major suppliers. It also established a risk management assessment for each of its major suppliers and created contingency plans for disaster planning at each location. Then, suppliers were trained in all of these planning elements. Finally, Nokia reevaluated its entire supply chain network to avoid single sourcing any major component, and it integrated these plans into its global sourcing strategies.[53]

Illustration 11: Nokia Ericsson Philips Event Timeline

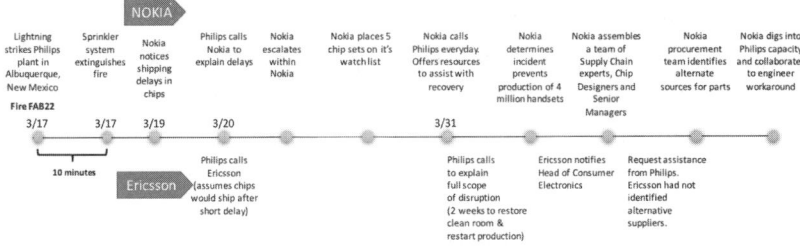

Illustration 12: Nokia Ericsson Impact

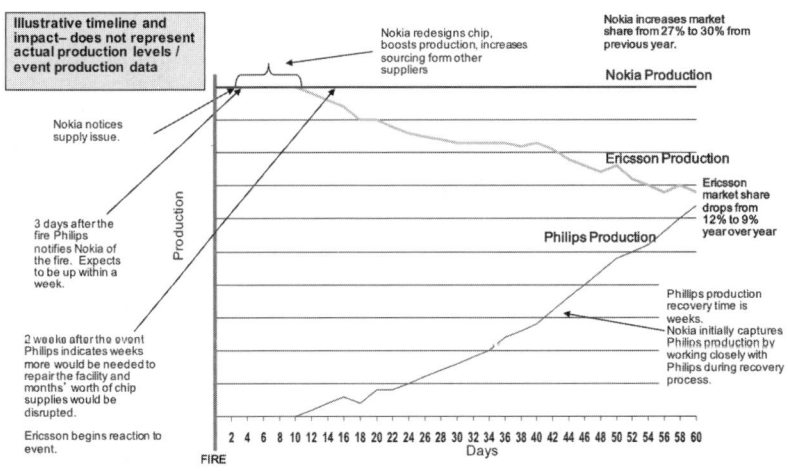

Development of visibility systems for tracking, even though designed as a reaction to the loss, was an example of how market advantage evolves when approached strategically. In this case, the single loss led to improved systems for improved future market advantage based

---

[53] Gary Lynch, *Single Point of Failure* (Hoboken, NJ: Wiley, 2009).

on the experience. The risk management procedure was expanded; uncertainty led to solutions, and those created improved processes and market advantage. The urgency in this case was apparent at once, so effective growth leadership demanded fast response, not only as a matter of risk mitigation, but also as a matter of creating market advantage.

Markets move fast, but organizations do not. However, in this case, Nokia conquered the tendency for slow reaction time with development of its shipping visibility systems. This was a case of applying urgency to manage uncertainty and create a smoother-working system.

Market advantage is best understood by analyzing what it means to an organization's stakeholders—customers, investors, strategic partners, competitors, regulators. These stakeholders have specific requirements imposed on growth leaders, who may be top executives of the company or other voices representing the organization.

Growth leaders are not merely expected to come up with creative solutions. In a majority of cases, market advantage results from thoughtful analysis of alternatives and picking the most reasonable path. When this is possible, the resulting market advantage might include an element of risk mitigation, not as a primary purpose, but as a happy consequence of thinking about uncertainty transformation. However, while thoughtful analysis is essential, it has to be created within this unavoidable urgency that is characteristic of uncertainty.

My early education about uncertainty and the urgency associated with it was perhaps somewhat unusual. However, early on I realized that markets and their actions were part of a broad uncertainty paradigm and that urgency was an intrinsic feature of this. When I landed at my career with Marsh, this became increasingly evident. I saw the trend as it evolved.

Marsh/Lexington/Zurich

As our innovative, value-based approach to understanding and measuring supply chain risk and uncertainty began to gain traction, notably after publication of my book, *Single Point of Failure*, so did increasing knowledge of how market interactions and interdependencies affected multiple tiers in a globally stretched supply chain. Besides creating, deploying, and refining a new capability, at Marsh we also accumulated a large amount of data that profiled these relationships and structural impacts to the industry and individual business operating models.

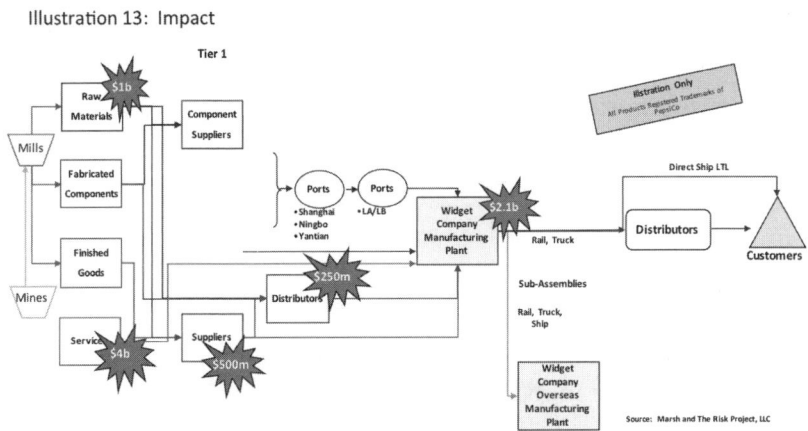

Illustration 13: Impact

As our success became widespread, Bob Howe, a visionary and one of the company's growth leaders, realized that there was value in this newfound set of competencies, capabilities, and mind-sets.

For Marsh, the risk management mind-set was apparent. Until this point, the market for supply chain insurance products and coverage was limited to physical property–related events (fires, floods, wind). Underwriters and their organizations were only willing to provide coverage that was predicated on a physical trigger, a natural or man-made hazard. These policies did not cover the failure of a supplier from nonphysical damage of events such as labor strikes, nationalization, or health events such as a pandemic.

The growth leader at Marsh suggested that we sit down with the underwriters from Lexington Insurance (part of AIG at the time) to see if we could provide enough insight and data to understand the impact of uncertainty throughout complex, interconnected supply chains. We had enough data to provide a degree of confidence. We had an opportunity to commercialize our process and data into a new insurance product. We had a distinct competencies, capabilities, and mind-sets at our disposal to accomplish this. Not only did we have the data, we also had the experience. We had experimented and gotten feedback, built analytical models, and developed specific training to gain greater site into uncertainty. This knowledge led to a financial product, an insurance policy for organization supply chains that provided up to $100 million in coverage. By purchasing the policy, organizations had the opportunity to better utilize the capital that they would normally spend on risk mitigation and investment. This became urgent once the nature of uncertainty was acknowledged and articulated.

The what-if could finally be answered since we had such tremendous insight into uncertainty. But in this case we took a proactive position, leveraged uncertainty, uncovered shared value, and created a brand-new product in the market that would provide us as well as the insurance carriers with market advantage. We reconciled the mind-sets of the stakeholders. This came about because of the insight offered by a visionary growth leader and a thorough understanding of uncertainty.

In our next case, that of Evonik, the change affected all industry participants (similar to the Xirallic paint pigment example in chapter 3), and if not addressed, it represented a structural failure in the industry. The industry as a whole failed to diversify a critical supplier. However, the uncertainty that grew from a common mode or single point of failure pointed the way to market advantage for others, if and only if, they responded at market speed. Clearly, urgency existed on two levels. First, the recovery period had to be managed and shortened as much as possible, and those who could potentially engineer or provide an alternative (Ube Industries and DuPont) would reap the market advantage benefits. Second, the uncertainty that grew from single-source supply chains revealed that in the future, the ability to outcompete, outgrow, and excel required a structural change and a smarter supplier network.

Evonik: Lighting the Fire

Here is a good example of an imposed change with focus on urgency. Evonik manufactures fire-retardant materials used in the airline, auto, and other industries. An explosion at Evonik's plant in Germany brought to light a serious supply issue. The entire industry relied on Evonik as the single supplier of a fire-retardant resin used in components in the auto industry. Reliance on a single supplier for any significant component in the primary product is always a threat to operations. If this can be resolved while gaining market advantage, it is the best possible outcome.

Recovery time was estimated at eighteen months. This brought together representatives from the auto industry to find alternatives immediately. This meeting highlighted possible solutions offered by DuPont and others.

> Executives from the world's largest automakers met today at a summit near Detroit to find alternative sources of resin used to make brake- and fuel-system components. The officials are searching for options after a March 31 explosion at chemical maker Evonik Industries AG halved the global source of an ingredient used to make the resin, called PA-12.
>
> Ube Industries, Asia's largest producer of the PA-12 resin used in cars, and DuPont Co. (DD), a maker of similar polymers, said order inquiries increased after the Evonik factory explosion. DuPont has been working with customers "to get a good sense of range of the magnitude of the issue and if we have alternative materials that might help," Carole Davies, a spokeswoman, said in an interview.[54]

---

[54] Craig Trudell and Mark Clothier, "Auto Output Threatened by Resin Shortage after Explosion," *Bloomberg*, April 17, 2012.

The fact that Evonik was the only supplier of an essential ingredient relied upon by the entire industry was only one part of the problem. Aggravating the problem further was that supplies were already short.

> The supply of PA-12 was already tight because it is also used in solar panels. In addition, Evonik says that it will take at least three months and perhaps longer before its damaged chemical plant can resume full production. That has set off alarm bells throughout the car industry.[55]

It might be said that the Evonik experience was an example of capitalism at its worst. The reliance on a single supplier may have had its origins in cost savings or parity, and that led to a possible disaster due to lack of diversification. Capitalism offers many benefits to progress; it also may have blind spots that actually prevent or subvert market advantage. Among those blind spots is a failure to recognize when a matter has become urgent. Who knew about this exposure? Were they prepared to convert this insight into market advantage (similar to the way Hyundai did in chapter 1)?

The growth leader welcomes uncertainty as part of the opportunity for making informed decisions. Evonik was able to exploit the urgency in this situation. Regardless of whether capitalism was at fault or not, the problem brought up issues that led to the potential to create market advantage. By identifying alternatives, the single-source supplier problem was solved through diversification. The availability of multiple sources for suitable replacements would be expected to reduce costs due to competition, a factor of capitalism that positively impacts how industries operate. The problem led to uncertainty, and resolving it was urgent. A second disaster would have been unacceptable.

In the auto industry, the shared value of needing to find alternatives was one version of a new trend. Another version of shared value

---

[55] Stephen Evans, "Fire in Small German Town Could Curb World Car Production," *BBC News,* April 19, 2012.

compares capitalism at its perceived worst with the possibility of creating social benefits. The urgency is most evident after a disaster, but the case is especially interesting when the response creates new market advantage. Vision-Ease was a case like this.

Shared value has yet another version worth bringing into the discussion. The entire auto industry had a shared value in finding alternatives to the single-source fire-retardant resin supplied by Evonik. By working together, they were able to overcome the urgent exposure associated with constrained or limited capacity. Shared value exists in virtually every case of market advantage creation. Without shared value, everyone suffers.

New ways of thinking are typical of uncertainty leaders, whether representing an entire industry and a single-source supplier or a chain of retail coffee outlets. A revolutionary way of thinking doesn't mean profitability should be ignored. It does mean that profitability is the result of creating and maintaining market advantage. Among these new ways of thinking is recognition of the urgency in competition itself. This new competitive landscape introduces new forms of urgency to organizations.

> The development of information and communication technologies and the globalization of industries have produced a blurring of industry boundaries that amounts to a massive reordering of business ... firms face significant uncertainty, ambiguity and an increasing number of strategic discontinuities ... Thus, managers are motivated to reduce the uncertainty by identifying new sources of competitive advantage.[56]

Exactly. These trends point out that acting on uncertainty is urgent, without exception. One company, upon analysis, discovered that its assumptions needed to be updated and even changed in some instances.

---

[56] Michael A. Hitt, Barbara W. Keats, and Samuel M. DeMarie, "Navigating in the New Competitive Landscape: Building Strategic Flexibility and Competitive Advantage in the 21st Century," *Academy of Management Executive,* December 1998.

It often occurs that a change is imposed, leading to action initiated. In other words, the case combines both types of change. This was the case for NVIDIA.

An Urgent and Uncertain Industry

In 2012, suppliers to the big high-tech OEMs found themselves barraged with endless streams of inquiries as to the viability of their businesses and their abilities to continue to supply them regardless of any change. One organization, NVIDIA, while completing the surveys realized that an aggressive posture on understanding and navigating uncertainty could lead to market advantage. NVIDIA decided to dig deep on the back end of its supply chain with the intention of ensuring that their assumptions were accurate and disruptions did not threaten its ability to supply the network. The company also explored the impact of disruptions to its competitors and the broader industry. A failure of an OEM or distributor could result in unwanted and expensive inventory. It discovered that many of its assumptions were misplaced or incomplete. The company manufactures graphics processing units (GPUs) for the mobile computing market, including Tegra® mobile processors for smartphones, tablets, and vehicular GPS systems.

The study involved a short list of key questions.

1. Where are we most at risk?
2. What have we done well?
3. How mature is our supply chain resiliency program?
4. How does our resiliency program compare to others?
5. Where should be consider taking action?

All of these issues relate to risk and, of course, to traditional risk management. However, rather than merely identifying areas at risk, this analysis revealed the current state of the system and its several uncertainties. By the way, given the concern with competition, all of these areas are also urgent.

Illustration 14: Participants in Back-end of GPU Supply Chain

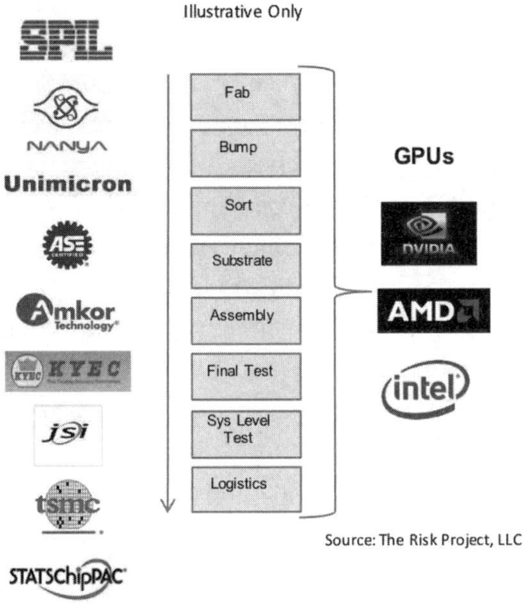

Illustrative Only

[Diagram showing supply chain participants: SPIL, NANYA, Unimicron, ASE, Amkor Technology, KYEC, JSI, tsmc, STATSChipPAC on the left; process steps Fab → Bump → Sort → Substrate → Assembly → Final Test → Sys Level Test → Logistics in the middle; GPUs (NVIDIA, AMD, intel) on the right.]

Source: The Risk Project, LLC

Part of the urgency was in logistics. Critical design, contracting, manufacturing, transportation, warehousing, and resource management were concentrated in four places: Santa Clara, California; Taiwan; Japan; and Hong Kong. This raised the question of resiliency and opportunity in the event of a major shock. Capacity for thin wafers was always at a premium due to the hyper competitiveness of the semiconductor industry. With three of the four centers of activity in Asia, events such as a catastrophic weather disaster could shut down most of the company's manufacturing and transportation network, as well as many other in the interconnected and interdependent supply chains. How long would it take to recover, replace, or move operations?

The problem was more than geographic. The company relied on only a few qualified plants and supply of essential materials. They also relied on a single transportation hub and shared key public infrastructure within the industry. This second level of risks defines the urgency

NVIDIA faced. To say the least, the company's assumptions about recovery and resilience were untested.

Four steps were needed to resolve the uncertainty of the resilience assumptions. First, diversification between Hong Kong and Santa Clara had to be expanded. Second, contingency plans (then in development) had to be finalized. Third, resources essential to the company had to be better diversified. And fourth, the company needed to improve its supplier knowledge, including development of collaborative working relationships, business reviews, and audits. This had to involve a review of planning and design policies, event monitoring, and programs to measure and monitor suppliers.

The objectives of this study were to determine when back-end companies were at the greatest vulnerability to a disruptive shock, analyze back-end supply chain resiliency programs and offer recommendations, and analyze scheduled backend suppliers in terms of their supply chain resiliency.

The results of NVIDIA's study were to address decreased levels of inventory diversification, which could lead to short-term material shortages; development of insights about other customers of the same suppliers (facing the same resiliency questions); a more evolved understanding at many levels, generated from demand as a starting point; and a better understanding of how to diversify the supplier base.

Under the traditional risk management approach, getting to the point of defining the scope of resiliency problems would have led to potential mitigation steps. This would include a judgment call about the likelihood of a negative impact in the case of a severe event. However, one aspect of the study was that it pointed out a broad range of uncertainties. It also provided suggestions about how to navigate that uncertainty, not in a reactive or preventive mode, but as a proactive approach to these issues. In other words, urgency itself could be transformed to create market advantage. With this mind-set, the company was able to overcome the uncertainties while reducing logistics and geographic risks.

However, this is also a case of adaptability. NVIDIA recognized that the world was far from certain or predictable. Acknowledging this volatile situation was urgent on its surface; it also clarified the need to a revise strategy based on the urgency of a rapidly changing world due to globalization and related volatility, changes in markets and how they function, and broad-based unpredictability across industries and international borders. By going through a supply chain resiliency analysis, collecting data, simulating navigation scenarios, and understanding recovery times, NVIDIA improved their risk profile as well as the market opportunity. Taking a page out of Cisco's resiliency book and with the assistance of event monitoring software, they immediately knew not only when something went "bump" in the night but also understood the implications.

There are lessons in these urgent, rapidly changing realities.

> All this uncertainty poses a tremendous challenge for strategy making. That's because traditional approaches to strategy – though often seen as the answer to change and uncertainty – actually assume a relatively stable and predictable world. Think about it. The goal of most strategies is to build an enduring (and implicitly static) competitive advantage … Companies undertake periodic strategy reviews and set direction and organizational structure on the basis of an analysis of their industry and some forecasts of how it will evolve … When change is so rapid, how can a one-year – or, worse, five-year – planning cycle stay relevant?[57]

In the case of NVIDIA, the growth leaders recognized this challenge and were able to change their logistical and geographic strategies to recognize evolving conditions. Urgency defines how uncertainty has only expanded over time.

---

[57] Martin Reeves and Mike Deimler, "Adaptability: The New Competitive Advantage," *Harvard Business Review,* July 2011.

Details: The Devil's in the Details, and This Demands Relentless Pursuit

A dramatic trend is under way among profit and loss leaders, product and brand category leaders, hedge fund managers, underwriters, and other growth leaders to identify effective methods of creating market advantage through the relentless pursuit of cause and effect. The key to exploiting uncertainty is based on who is looking at it to make decisions, who is affected, and their ability to zoom in to the details and zoom out to the "big picture." A growth leader creates and acts on opportunities, including the ecosystem and its behaviors that deliver value to market. The question is, how do big picture cause and effect impact material, market-moving situations, and what decisions have to follow?

What did all of the case histories introduced in prior chapters have in common? What details matter most? For Nokia, they noticed shipping delays before their competitors (market); Hyundai realized their larger competitors would move slowly, so he focused on understanding uncertainty and rapid execution (market/competitors); Roche understood the uncertainty details about a new commercial buyer, regulators, inventory management, and the entire value chain and what their competitors had the capability to do (market/leaders/managers).

This is a key question because as a growth leader, you need to identify the traits other leaders have in common. One action that they all took was to do a 360-size-up of the situation they faced. When firefighters first arrive on the scene of a fire call, they walk around the building to develop a complete understanding of the situation—any victims hanging out the window, location of the fire, life and safety hazards, access paths. To gain market advantage, you use the same tactic; analyze the entire situation analytically, thoughtfully, and thoroughly. You take an outsider point of view. To have a 360 understanding of your market (customers, investors, strategic partners, regulators, competitors) as it relates to the specific situation (change + decisions + assumptions), the first step is to understand the market first and then other positions, perspectives, and interests of leaders and managers. Dan Pengue, former chief risk officer, vendor finance, GE Capital, summed the need to understand uncertainty from a market vantage point as follows.

> If my competitor suddenly was able to get inventory turns up to 4.6 from prior year of 4.2 but did so by ignoring or not understanding the details of uncertainty than that was an opportunity for us. Investors always want to know that you are running a prudently, well-disciplined organization with no surprises (in fact that's what investor relations does on a daily basis, provide the facts and keep them informed). I needed to leverage my market advantage of knowing (competencies and capabilities), i.e. I thoroughly understood the risk to my supply and value chains as well as understood the implications, i.e. the impact to cash flow and other key performance metrics, to a disruption. We needed to positon, brainstorm and plan on how to capitalize on the rainy day since I knew that my competitor was potentially facing market cap erosion exposure because they did not

know about constraints, leverage by others or linkages that were not so obvious (e.g. hedge fund example). My inventory turns might not have kept pace but oh boy, if there is blip we are going to pounce on the opportunity. Successful risk leaders figure out early on how to manage risk - not avoid it. It's easy to say no. As a risk leader in GE Capital finding ways to support and drive profitable growth while maintaining portfolio stability and minimizing losses was just your job. If you refused to accept the challenge, someone else would.

This is what our growth leaders had in common in every case history. It is the set of common traits, the not only of what you face but all of the aspects of uncertainty that you need to address and turn to market advantage. The most significant principle if you truly want to gain market advantage is about the execution. If the goal is to gain market advantage—meaning in regard to the customer, the competition, investors, regulatory system, and strategic partners—you must understand how the details apply.

What does this mean? Rockwell Automation is a publicly traded firm that produces industrial automation products. The company markets products such as control systems, motor control devices, sensors, and industrial control panels. Rockwell markets its products in eighty countries, generates approximately $6.3 billion in sales, and employees more than 22,000 people.[58]

Its leaders and managers wanted to understand uncertainty because an issue arose. The company simply didn't know what parts and suppliers were most critical in the complexity of its delivery systems. This concern drove Brad Phillips, director of strategic sourcing, and his team at Rockwell to create a material risk index (MRI) and component resiliency index (CRI). This also drove real-time crisis monitoring, 3rd party supplier assessments, pre-established business priorities, predictive analytics, and

---

[58] http://www.rockwellautomation.com/global/about-us/company-profile.page.

a disruption "playbook". All were linked to the product. The net result was development of an understanding of uncertainty at the product level.

The Figure describes Rockwell's analysis of this uncertainty with highlights in the details.

Illustration 15: Rockwell Automation Filtering Process

	TIER 1	TIER 2	TIER 3
Company Suppliers	An inventory of ALL SUPPLIERS	Value segmentation and tiering process yields a subset, referred to as MANDATORY SUPPLIERS	Further refinement of criticality, via the value segmentation process yields a top tier list of suppliers, referred to as CRITICAL SUPPLIERS
Parts Top SKU component parts			
Suppliers Preferred suppliers	All Product Families All Products	Subset of Product Families & Subset of Products	Subset of Product Families & further subset of Products (e.g. Top 50 products)
Markets Raw material or market capacity		Value Driver Filter Revenue, margin, brand, regulatory, and/or strategic filter applied to prioritize suppliers by product families	

Source: Rockwell Automation

Criteria to evaluate this issue included culture, readiness, business model, resiliency, and estimated total time to recover in the event of a loss upstream. Rockwell originally created a MRI. The MRI preceded the CRI and was mainly used as a proactive obsolescence tool. This was built on the same concept, but the output went to material engineering. The next phase of evolution was a conversation with engineering. The high risk was identified at 4 percent of the thousands of parts required for processes. This was a high risk level, so Rockwell's leaders and managers decided to identify the highest priority parts.

> Material Risk Index (MRI) Analysis: Proactive obsolescence indicator tool for components. Utilizes input from external sources and suppliers as part of algorithm to score components.

> Component Resiliency Index (CRI) Analysis: Proactive identification tool for components (and factored products) that have a higher potential risk of disruption of supply in the event of a crisis. Utilizes feedback from suppliers on their business continuity planning (BCP) practices.

The need for deep, ongoing insight and technical knowledge about their extended supply chain partners motivated Rockwell to acquire a third party event monitoring software tool (at the time of the printing of this book the leaders in this space included: Resilinc EventWatch™, NC4 RiskCenter™, Kinaxis RapidResponse™). The company began monitoring external products. It monitored hazards, geo-politics, and a dozen other events by supplier location. A total of 2,000 individual locations in fifty countries were studied and matched to the CRI database which includes 77,000 parts.

The innovation phase and market advantage began with an understanding of when the engineering of new products could reduce risk up front, achieve greater efficiency, and potentially build market advantage. This is where the uncertainty advantage kicked in. Once the pinpoint for improved efficiency was identified, Rockwell was able to convert uncertainty into a clear market advantage.

Case Study: Tomorrow's Details, Midsized Industrial Case

In some cases, analysis of suppliers in great detail is necessary to gain the uncertainty advantage. In other instances, focus has to be on value creation.

The following example demonstrates how the CEO (leader) of a midsized industrial manufacturing company gained market advantage in this way. Its customer was a global industrial supply company that distributed industrial products including motors, lighting, material handling, fasteners, plumbing, tools, and safety supplies. The customer managed its supply side risk by diversifying its sourcing between two main providers. After many years of a nearly even split, the competitor decided it was time to gain greater market advantage by reducing the price of their products by 20 percent, which required a structural change. It was a risky move since there was no turning back. Once the lower product catalog was offered, the buyer would expect that this price would be permanent.

The competitor believed it could achieve a 30 percent reduction in cost of goods sold by migrating manufacturing of the product to Mexico. The majority of that savings could be returned to its customers, and as a result the company could capture another 5 percent to 15 percent market share. What typically happens in this situation is the competing company would match the move and the savings, further commoditizing the market (and in doing so, potentially lowering the barrier to entry for competitors). However, the CEO took a different strategy by navigating uncertainty in the decision to gain market share and protect already thin margins. This demanded great attention to the details.

The CEO knew that he needed to thoroughly understand and quantify the potential opportunity and performance impact of uncertainty over a three- to five-year time horizon. First, the investment needed to migrate capacity to Mexico was quantified, and the performance expectation was established. Next, uncertainty was introduced into the equation and analyzed over the same period. Finally, data was collected, and the risk of the uncertainty for each scenario was modeled to restate what the anticipated performance expectation.

The result of analyzing uncertainty early in the value creation process revealed that the reduction in price was not sustainable by either his or his competitor's company. Over a very short period, the market advantage would evaporate and create a bigger price margin issue. Significant and rapidly increasing expense would be incurred in order to manage risk in a newly configured supply chain. For example, additional overhead would be incurred throughout the product life cycle in order to manage a variety of regulatory, environmental, asset, security, and safety risks.

Another concern arose as a result of stress testing the new supply chain. The analysis revealed a significant increase in the probability of a business disruption. The savings would evaporate in eight months, and either the buyer—or worse, the CEO's organization—would have to absorb the extra expense or exit the business. The CEO shared the results of the analysis with the buyer and leveraged them as market advantage. He requested that the buyer challenge the competitor on how they would sustain their business with this extra expense. Would quality be spared?

The Detailed Landscape of Uncertainty

As the previous case reveals, analysis of the details often leads to an informed decision that might not be discovered otherwise. The complexity of just about any situation points to the importance of the details within the landscape of uncertainty.

Gaining a complete picture of uncertainty and how it affects the organization is not a simple task. It exists on so many levels and has so many ramifications that the navigation itself demands a careful and broad view of the entire process. The well-known model of enterprise risk management (ERM) has not effectively addressed methods for decision-making. It is widely agreed that failure rates are high. Why is this? In my opinion, it is not just failure in decisions but failure to take action that defines the failure of traditional ERM. With management focusing on reactive risk management, motivated by operational, financial, and compliance as the drivers of change, you have to expect a big failure rate. Putting this another way was industry expert John Kotter.

> From years of study, I estimate today more than 70 percent of needed change either fails to be launched, even though some people clearly see the need, fails to be completed, even though some people exhaust themselves trying, or finishes over budget, late and with initial expectations unmet.[59]

---

[59] Cited by J. Lam, "Risk Management: The ERM Guide from AFP," *Association for Financial Professionals*, 2011.

A symptom of the focus within ERM on risk as a driver of decisions within organizations comes at the expense of market-driven concepts. The debate centers of whether focus should be on financial risk or operational risk, with little to no regard for markets and the uncertainty advantage. As one author explained,

> If the goal of ERM is to enable management to identify, prioritize, and manage risk, ERM programs ought to focus first on strategic risks, followed by operational risks. The financial risks that dominate ERM today should come a distant third. ERM professionals have focused on financial risks because they are easy to quantify and universally applicable.[60]

This focus on risk is at the core of the problem and demonstrates why cause and effect are matters for uncertainty navigation, not risk management. The entire discussion of strategic risk is legitimate, but it belongs in the function of operational offices run by risk managers as part of the normal set of nonmarket activities. The growth leader should not be funneled into these financial and operational concerns but should focus instead on market-driven cause and effect and the steps needed to create market advantage.

The same article provided an excellent definition of risk management as an operational process involving a study of the details.

> Risk management is a dynamic process in which information flows from line managers up to senior managers who monitor progress and, when necessary, develop action plans and send instructions back down to line managers.[61]

---

[60] J. Lam, "Strategic Risk Management: The next frontier for ERM," *Workiva*, February 2015.
[61] Ibid.

The definition is on point but only as the operational process that risk management should be. None of this has anything to do with the cause and effect of market-driven initiatives. In fact, risk management can and should support market-driven programs, not as a primary source for decisions, but as one of many causes for affecting change. In one case, this applied to a compliance question and led to transformation of the organizational resiliency program.

The importance of details in another case—Huntsman—makes the point.

Huntsman Case

From the company's website:

> Huntsman is a global manufacturer and marketer of differentiated chemicals. Our operating companies manufacture products for a variety of global industries, including chemicals, plastics, automotive, aviation, textiles, footwear, paints and coatings, construction, technology, agriculture, health care, detergent, personal care, furniture, appliances and packaging. Originally known for pioneering innovations in packaging and, later, for rapid and integrated growth in petrochemicals, Huntsman has approximately 15,000 employees and operates from multiple locations worldwide. The Company had 2015 revenues of over $10 billion.[62]

The company acquired CIBA's specialty chemical business for $250 million several years ago. The appreciation of the Swiss franc had significantly disrupted the cost structure (nearly 30 percent appreciation against the US dollar in an eight-month period). Operating in a razor-thin margin industry and with approximately 50 percent of the cost

---

[62] www.huntsman.com.

of operating the business tied to the Swiss franc, the time had come to take aggressive action to fundamentally improve financial performance. The CEO, Peter Huntsman, summed up the opportunity with the following statement: "We've made extensive and costly efforts to boost this division's competitiveness since acquiring the Business in 2006, but as customers and competitors moved their centers of business to Asia, we must re-align ourselves according to industry trends." [63]

The assumption was that closing the plant in Switzerland and transferring more than five hundred products elsewhere would result in an annual cost savings in the neighborhood of 15 to 30 million USD. Moving operations elsewhere would also expand capabilities globally, especially in the Asian market, where many suppliers and customers were located.

This was an opportunity to enhance performance, improve the cost structure, and expand into new markets, all of which presented a very attractive business opportunity. Now the risk questions. How fast can the transfer and shutdown occur, and what uncertainty and obstacles can slow us down or jeopardize our opportunity to achieve the cost savings and expansion expectations? And which ones should we pay the most attention to, measure, and mitigate? Who owns the intellectual property? Are the permits correct (do they reflect chemistry and technologies, in countries with increasing sensitivity to environmental exposure)? What's the lead time on product registration? Do we have all the data from our suppliers? Knowing these details is what enables the knowledge to be leveraged. Did their competitors understand and have the information about the issues? Did any of these issues serve as a "barrier" for Huntsman's competitors?.

This was a case of identifying cause and effect by looking at the issues through the detail lens of the uncertainty advantage. The leadership team had the collective competency and inherent capability to be sure they understood uncertainty as part of their growth strategy. They

---

[63] www.huntsman.com press release, "Huntsman Announces Significant Restructuring at its Textile Effects Business in Basel, Switzerland"

set an expectation and instead of charging off without analysis, they dug deep to reveal and minimize uncertainty to maintain market position.

In another case, that of Rana Plaza, a disaster pointed out that outsourcing to get cheap labor creates a different kind of cause and effect. This is especially true when standards in the source country are not controlled or regulated carefully.

Rana Plaza: A Lesson in the Details and Related Cause and Effect

The garment industry went through several massive outsourcing shifts, the most recent when workers' wages began climbing in China and elsewhere. In 2013, a worker earned approximately $1.26 an hour in China, whereas a worker in Bangladesh earned 24 cents an hour. Prudent decision makers stepped on the gas and tried to gain the uncertainty advantage over each other. However, the environment in Bangladesh presented a great deal of uncertainty and required a much closer look before signing the contracts. Bangladesh is a risky place to conduct business due to poor building codes, political unrest, high frequency of adverse weather, nonexistent labor laws, and other reasons. When faced with the opportunity to perform, decision makers did not pay close attention to the potential consequences of moving operations solely to increase profit margins. The true cause and effect was ignored.

All appeared to be okay even though uncertainty was not seriously considered. Then, in April 2013, a building collapsed at Rana Plaza, killing more than 1,100 workers. By this point, the uncertainty advantage had disappeared since the majority of the industry had concentrated an industry in a single geographic region. Aside from the human tragedy, the industry took it on the chin as well. The collective bias drove the major retailers to the same decision, sourcing from Bangladesh. Over the years, the industry had lost a great deal of leverage over variable costs. Labor was one of the few remaining leverage points, with Bangladesh providing labor at one-fifth the cost of China. This appeared to be an opportunity without a downside, but only because the details were not carefully studied. As a result, Bangladesh in 2013 quickly became the third-biggest exporter of clothes in the world, after China and Italy. There were five thousand factories in the country, employing 3.6 million garment workers. Manufacturers had easy access to cheap raw materials.[64]

When faced with the opportunity to improve margins, the decision makers did not even consider the potential cause and effect of a profit-based motive. When faced with the decision to continue forward, lower cost, grow, and stay relevant in the market via aggressive pricing or do the analysis, consider uncertainty and alter expectations to reflect reality, the decision makers went for performance improvement without analysis.

Competitors claimed to be able to drastically lower prices, but that came with a catch. Could market advantage be gained if one the major players chose to understand uncertainty and factor it into the change cycle? Lacking this approach, most had to deal with consequences only when the risk was realized.

Details reveal the truth. When the obvious and apparent benefits of cost-cutting are as far as the study goes, the larger picture is simplified, often at great cost. Market advantage is developed not with profit motive and cost-cutting alone. Ironically, moving away from traditional risk management and toward uncertainty advantage prevents many risks from occurring in the first place. This is where the details matter.

---

[64] Jonathan Fahey and Anne d'Innocenzio, "Retailers Face Tough Decisions after Bangladesh Factory Collapse," *Associated Press*, May 12, 2013.

Priority: Growth Trumps Risk

Markets think about value, leaders think about growth, and managers think about performance and risk. These are individual priorities, understandably. There is a hierarchy requiring acknowledgment that growth drives the process. But without reconciling these priorities, they get out of sequence or operate independently and in conflict with one another. Leaders such as Bezos at Amazon, Zuckerberg at Facebook, Musk at Tesla and Space-X, Ellison at Oracle, and Jobs at Apple had a common attribute. They put growth first and also reconciled disparate interests. Your priority is to recognize not only the aggregate but the individual drivers of growth and uncertainty.

Growth will always trump risk if there is significant benefit to be gained. It may take some time, but growth will always prevail. Uncertainty may delay its realization, but if the market potential is large enough, growth will eventually prevail. Examples of this phenomenon include what once was perceived as risky ventures such as the Internet, social networks, mobile computing, personal computers on every desktop, the industrial Internet, nanotechnology, streaming video, driverless cars, and 3D printing. If you believe in this hypothesis, why not pursue risk and uncertainty with the same mind-set and persistency as growth, recognizing the opportunity to gain advantage?

Growth Trumps Risk Strategically

Success breeds complacency. In this regard, during times of certainty and safety, no real progress occurs because there is no need to change anything. One case of a company refusing to become complacent was a producer of a multibillion dollar drug used to treat the symptoms of psychotic conditions such as schizophrenia and bipolar, Otsuka Pharmaceutical Development & Commercialization Corporation.

From the company's website:

> Established in 1964, Otsuka Pharmaceutical is a total healthcare company. In keeping with its corporate philosophy of 'Otsuka - people creating new products for better health worldwide,' it aims to treat illness and sustain day-to-day well-being. With a pharmaceutical business that provides breakthrough treatments for patients around the world, and a nutraceutical business that helps healthy people get even healthier, Otsuka Pharmaceutical researches, develops, produces and sells highly innovative and creative products.[65]

This philosophy was applied in a way that resiliency was assessed and measured by the company's auditors (compliance/rules/standards strategy). The leaders did not believe the process gave them a true picture of uncertainty and the opportunity that may exist if significant disruptions were presented to the business model. The executive leaders and board, led by their CFO and vice president of technical operations, refused to adopt a mind-set of growth independent of risk or

---

[65] http://www.otsuka.com.

visa-versa. They believed they needed to avoid the success pitfalls, such as complacency and arrogance, in the belief that prior success negated the need to dig deep and relentlessly pursue uncertainty. Little did they know that their mind-sets toward the need for continuously uncovering vulnerabilities to their multibillion dollar blockbuster drug would also lead to greater operating efficiencies and market confidence. In other words, growth became the driving force, and risk management (in its traditional definition) was a following attribute. The leaders, CFO and global head of technical operations, avoided the norm, which would consist of checklists and surveys for understanding risk. This was a challenge to the compliance/rules-based risk strategy that had been recommended by the external audit firm. They believed that it just hadn't gone far enough and did not align with the market need. The CFO raised the question, if the patient and the product availability, quality, efficacy, and cost is what we care about most than why wouldn't our risk and uncertainty strategy begin there as well? He also questioned whether the strategy should be based on the just the physical asset, a checklist item, and why would be so myopic and view the supply chain just from an IT or facility perspective.

Clearly, they were seeking guidance that applied directly to the patient and the product from beginning to end. How does the organization ensure that patient is getting the high quality drug regardless of the circumstance throughout the supply chain? How do we ensure that the brand stays relevant in the market if there were an interruption? How do we ensure that the product does not get displaced by a generic provider if we experience a business disrupiton? As a result of this analysis, the executives and leadership team ordered a thorough analysis of the entire multibillion dollar product life cycle. They needed to understand what they did not know as well as how the information they gained could be leveraged into the critical decision-making during uncertain or opportunistic times.

The leaders pursued uncertainty with simple questions such as, what would be the impact of disruptive change to our business? Examples included market or structural change, new product innovation, medical or adverse product event, fire, flood, loss of key active product ingredient (API) or excipient supplier, and natural or man-made hazards. They defined it as any circumstance that could disrupt the flow of their blockbuster drug (in UTA terms this is the "situation"). They went on to ask what the market, regulatory, and operational behaviors would be as a result of a disruption. They believed absence of their blockbuster, multibillion dollar drug in the market for an extended period would result in a threat to their patients and a potential loss of revenue, market share, and brand value. Assuming that a large percentage of scripts were written by doctors affiliated with price-sensitive, government-funded programs, from a competitive point of view (the generic manufacturers), their concern was simple. If for some reason they could not get their premium-priced quality drug to their patients, an alternative would be provided in short order.

Although switching from one schizophrenia or bi-polar drug has significant potential side effects, the alternative was worse. And for Otsuka, if the drug were not available in the market for an extended period time and a generic was the only alternative, there was a possibility that the business might never return to Otsuka. As a result, management believed that physicians would be forced to use a generic version. If that were the case, the drug would probably sell for a fraction of the current price, the cause and effect of the consequences of taking no action. If the alternative drug were to have positive patient results, the chance of permanent displacement was a reality. The list of possibilities for disruption was endless including: a recall or quality issue, manufacturing glitch, transportation delays or strikes, regulatory oversight, weather event, or even a mishap with the packaging, kitting, or labeling. The generic drug producers could gain an irreversible uncertainty advantage, and the original producer would be displaced in the market. Pedal to the metal, as they say, and advantage goes to generics.

The big difference with Otsuka's was how they addressed the uncertainty faced by these questions. A more popular and traditional approach might have been to enjoy market domination while it lasted, hoping it would last indefinitely. But Otsuka was not willing to simply address the known risks in the traditional, reactive manner. Their goal was to reconcile growth and uncertainty mind-sets. By tackling uncertainty to ensure growth, the company recognized the basic fact that growth trumps risk.

What were the lessons learned? Otsuka leveraged uncertainty to create a clear market advantage, applying value-driven strategy to understanding uncertainty throughout the supply chain (they mapped the entire supply chain). This meant growth-based changes from active ingredient and raw material production and sourcing in Asia through production in Latin America to packaging and wholesale distribution in the United States. They conducted a thorough end-to-end analysis (raw material through patient medication), collected detailed data about the flows and critical resources, modeled failure points, and strategies for risk mitigation and financing.

The leaders and managers also asked about the capabilities of their competitors. It appeared all adopted a compliance or rules-based strategy. Although it appeared that a performance-based strategy was being applied, it turned out by gaining a deep understanding of the extended flows and business models used at all stages that they could better anticipate and predict. This was a clear uncertainty advantage if the transformation succeeded. They applied rapid prototype of value-driven solution to a $6 billion blockbuster drug supply chain; designed an extensive supplier risk program; analyzed more than two dozen of their largest business partners (manufacturers, excipient suppliers, labs, and clinical research organizations); and provided comprehensive product, material, financial, and information flow maps of the extended value chains for two blockbuster drugs. They quantified and qualified risk exposure at all critical points in the value chain. Next they defined an inventory risk strategy and created ongoing advisory services to the CEO, board, CFO, and chief technical/supply chain officer.

All of these steps were part of a method to retool not only the processes but the attitude as well. It was not enough to manufacture a high-quality product. To hold onto market share, Otsuka recognized that it needed to tighten the supply chain so that growth was a natural evolution of everything else they had done.

Unleashing the Uncertainty Advantage and Market-Driven Mind-Set

Are you a hard-charging growth leader who often encounters naysayers or managers who create obstacles to prevent rapid deployment of your initiatives? Do you often find yourself at the mercy of assessments, audits and surveys, third-party reviews, and checking the box? You might be of the mind-set that the intention of these generic risk activities and programs are valid but not relevant or do not yield value. As a result, you may find yourself enlisting others to uncover a workaround, or maybe you just apply brute force to plow right through the obstacle. If you are a manager with either direct or indirect risk-related responsibilities (in operations, IT, compliance, audit, legal, insurance, operations, or program management), do you often find yourself exhibiting defensive actions, present negative arguments, or have a value preservation mind-set? Do you find yourself at odds with growth leaders, believing that they should pay a bit more attention to how risk is being managed?

Growth and risk will always be in conflict. However, a market-driven strategy and an uncertainty advantage mind-set can provide a common purpose, especially if it's defined in the context of the market, a situation and its priorities. Threat, compliance, and performance strategies and programs are not designed to gain this insight. For threat- or event-based strategies, the growth agenda is not designed as an integral part of the strategy. As a result, the overriding mission is to return to normal as quickly and as efficiently as possible. Insurance is viewed this way. Its purpose is to smooth volatility rather than to allow the leader to step on the gas.

Compliance- or rules-based strategies seldom take the growth agenda into consideration. These strategies are designed to get the organization and its processes in sync with a standard that is often defined by a regulatory body, industry peer group, audit group, or contract. There is no mention of enablement of the growth agenda. Performance-based strategies move the discussion a bit closer to the market but usually in the context of margin rather than growth and innovation. Typically applied by managers, performance-based strategies can potentially be leveraged as a market differentiator if the gains are substantial and sustainable. Performance is best driven in terms of setting priorities for growth, profitability, liquidity, and leverage. In theory, these four should be viewed holistically. In practice, conflicting agendas and individual priorities simply get in the way and prevent the ideal from becoming the reality. What we all need is a better parachute. In practical terms, the parachute is not intended to prevent us from landing or even to slow down the landing but to fall as quickly as possible without injury. Illustration 16 summarizes how priorities during times of growth are viewed under four strategic models.

Illustration 16: Comparison of Strategies

Characteristics	Threat/Event/FUD	Compliance/Rules	Performance/Asset	Market
Mindset	• Driven by event • *Manager* • Manage • Reactive • Little MS reconciliation • Urgency x Risk = Exposure • View - obstacle • Preserve & stabilize value • Situation based •	• Driven by regulators, rule-makers • *Manager* • Manage • Reactive • Little MS reconciliation/dictated • Likelihood x Impact = Exposure • View - obstacle • Preserve value • Organization/governance based	• Driven by Operations & Finance • *Manager* • Manage • Proactive/Reactive • Little MS reconciliation/return • Impact x Effort = Return • View- obstacle & performance differentiator • Preserve value • Measurement based	• Driven by the Market • *Leader* • Navigate • Proactive • Reconcile mindsets • Uncertainty x Urgency = Opportunity • View - Opportunity & differentiator • Create value • Situation based
Competencies	• Combination thinking	• Deductive thinking	• Deductive thinking	• Inductive thinking
Capabilities	• Mapping (only within scope of event), monitoring • Event based allocation of risk resources • Risk methods: qualitative, gut, experience, instinct	• Comparative, surveying, program-based • Program based allocation of risk resources (ERM, others) • Risk methods: qualitative, scorecards, heat maps, likelihood/impact grids, surveys	• Mapping, impact (*Manager*), modeling • Portfolio based allocation of risk resources (performance driven) • Risk methods: qualitative, decision analysis theory (probabilistic & deterministic), scenario	• Mapping, impact (*Market, Leader, Manager*), Listening posts • Portfolio based allocation of risk resources (market driven) • Risk methods: qualitative, decision analysis theory (probabilistic & deterministic), scenario

SOURCE: The Risk Project, LLC

The figure aptly compares the different levels of attitude and how priorities are set or ignored. Under FUD, apprehension immobilizes management, and any growth leader has the daunting task of overcoming resistance. In the compliance model, management is given over to regulation, and the attitude becomes one of following the rules without consideration of markets. Under the performance model, focus is on ever-higher profits, so management is motivated to avoid any and all risks that could threaten the bottom line. This means market initiative has to be discouraged and given zero priority. Finally, in the market-driven model, priority is given to growth. Remember, growth trumps risk, and in this model, change and uncertainty are embraced as opportunities.

If you are a manager, we are talking about how to support the decision not to be the decision.

To gain market advantage, the following principles may be applied.

- A market-driven strategy for navigating uncertainty requires the reconciliation the market, leader, and manager mind-sets.
- The growth leader navigates uncertainty as part of change for a given situation. The situational context is used to focus business decisions, assumptions, and expected outcomes.
- Not all change will justify the investment in the market (uncertainty) advantage strategy. Other strategies include threat-based (or FUD/fear, uncertainty, doubt), compliance/rules-based, or performance-based value preservation strategies for managing risk and uncertainty.

In some cases, a difficult challenge is presented unexpectedly, and a company with a market mind-set reacts perfectly by turning it into a positive attribute. The following case makes this point.

Johnson & Johnson and the Original Tylenol Contamination

When you understand uncertainty, you are rewarded, and it's not always about an immediate growth opportunity. You establish market advantage via better, faster, and more accurate decision-making. This means developing more precise anticipation and response to the market; developing market precision and agility; and focusing on greater customer, investor, and regulator confidence and trust.

Here's a case where growth trumped risk, not by natural design, but by natural effect. It came about because the organization decided to respond to a specific circumstance by understanding uncertainty. They acted on and navigated to create advantage. In the widely publicized

Tylenol cyanide contamination, the product was compromised, the market lost confidence, and the product was lost because it had to be taken off the shelves. The big challenge to Johnson & Johnson was how to preserve the brand, not to mention preserving the company. Tylenol was a huge revenue generator. At the time of this incident, it was the best-selling painkiller medicine with 35 percent market share.

The initial big decision was whether or not to recall. The markets of uncertainty, capabilities, competencies, and mind-sets led to the obviously right decision to recall all of the product nationally at an estimated cost of $100 million. The company recognized that its responsibility was to those who used Johnson & Johnson products and services, an attitude that applies to all situations. The standard is to reveal all you know as fast as you can. It's the only way to be certain to preserve brand and reputation.

The overall outcome was that the cost of the recall turned out to be a huge market advantage. Johnson & Johnson was recognized as a company that did the right thing without hesitation. The risk element—the cost of the recall—paled in comparison to the company's reputation in the market.

Chrysler: Identifying the Strategic Partners

In another example, the organization needed to better understand its risk universe before it discovered how to establish priorities.

Between 2002 and 2014, sales at Chrysler were growing in double digits. A merger with Fiat strengthened overall revenues and earnings, and focus was on financial and operational excellence. However, the focus on strategic risk ignored what should have been a key priority within this growth period: the role of the company's suppliers.

What Chrysler had not yet learned was a simple but profound truth; strategic partners are market drivers, too. This talent is not solely owned by the home office.

This is a common problem. Companies focusing on profits tend to see suppliers as adversaries and seek price reductions. Ironically, this attitude reduces supplier trust, which in turn reduces supplier willingness to give price concessions. The outcome ends up the opposite of what the company wants, and this is exactly what happened at Chrysler. Trust levels fell off between 2006 and 2009, and price concessions tracked reduced trust levels in the same period.

This raises a strategic risk aspect to growth. When management focuses on profits and growth leadership is not a priority, the results suffer. An automotive study revealed that the more companies trusted their suppliers, the greater the benefits realized. These soft benefits provided by suppliers include a willingness to share new product information, investment in future customer needs, willingness to allocate resources to support customers, and improved communication. The survey was revealing.

> ... we found that the financial contribution of the soft benefits suppliers provide Chrysler are, like supplier price concessions, highly correlated with supplier trust. In addition, the value of these non-price contributions greatly and consistently exceeds the monetary value of the suppliers' price concessions.[66]

The implication here is that when growth priorities are focused on financial considerations, more permanent aspects of growth may be ignored. The strategic risk of alienating suppliers is a deterioration of growth itself and, ironically, ends up costing future profits. The study estimated that the decline in supplier trust levels ended up costing $24 billion in profits over twelve years, in spite of the company's financial motives to cut costs and make bigger profits. As the authors concluded,

> These outcomes suggest that companies that pressure suppliers in an adversarial manner to obtain greater

---

[66] John W. Henke Jr., Thomas T. Stallkamp, and Sengun Yeniyurt, "Lost Supplier Trust, Lost Profits," *Supply Chain Management Review*. May/June 2014.

price concessions to improve their bottom line are, in fact, doing themselves a great disservice.[67]

Although Chrysler has taken steps to improve relations with suppliers, trust levels remain lower than they were in the 1990s. Two lessons explaining this aspect of growth are (1) building trust with stakeholders is not only smart strategy risk, it is also smart financial responsibility; and (2) building trust with suppliers leads to enhancement of other concessions, thus greater profits. That's where the priority should be—not in risk reduction or better margins, but in growth based on mutual trust and respect.

Case History: Performance at Uncertainty, Focus on Turning Loss to Advantage

At the time, the largest cyberattack ever recorded was the case of TJX Companies, in which private information (especially credit card account data) was stolen in a breach of the company's system over a period extending from July 2005 until its discovery in December 2006. In such a case, what are the priorities, and how do they get set?

TJX is the largest global off-price apparel retailer, with 3,300 stores in the United States, Canada, and Europe. Among its holdings are Marshall's, T.J. Maxx, and several smaller retail chains. TJX works with 450 buyers and over 10,000 vendors worldwide.[68] On discovery of the breach, the immediately identified losses were an unknown number of customer credit card account numbers. The immediate impacts were anticipated as loss of credit card customers, an increase in cash transactions, and long-term reduced confidence in retail security systems.

TJX benefitted from this incident in spite of perceptions that the event was largely a negative. Among the steps TJX took as forms of setting priorities based on uncertainty were

---

[67] Ibid.
[68] https://www.tjx.com/business/.

- Immediate disclosure of the problem
- Aggressive program of discounts to customers as well as sales programs
- Dismissal or settlement of lawsuits, perceived by the market as good news
- Replacement of the CEO
- Accelerated advertising and marketing campaigns

The outcomes from these steps included

- Increases in the customer base and revenues
- Perception of TJX not as at fault but as a victim along with customers
- Increases in TJX stock prices over the twelve months following disclosure

    The positive outcomes should not ignore the short-term losses the company suffered and potential losses to customers whose accounts were compromised. However, by seeking the advantage in this situation, TJX created positive outcomes by enacting performance at uncertainty. The uncertainty included unknown levels of credit card breaches, customer reactions to the retail stores and their security, market reactions reflected in stock prices, and what disclosure would cause. The point in this lesson is that growth occurs in many ways, and the real risk in this case was not limited to the financial losses due to the cyberattack but the more significant potential loss of company reputation as a consequence. This was a problem similar to that faced by Johnson & Johnson. In a similar manner, TJX took steps to minimize the impact to its customers while confronting the issue head-on.

    Although the experience was daunting and the losses potentially catastrophic, a simple truth emerged. Coming clean and telling the truth as quickly as possible not only mitigates the damage but, ironically, creates growth in unexpected ways. This was a case of something going wrong and then a conversion of the uncertainty into a growth opportunity.

By setting priorities for the steps that could be taken (replacement of the CEO, sales and discount offers, advertising and marketing campaigns, and rapid dismissal or settlement of lawsuits), TJX appeared to be trying to maximize uncertainty in the most positive way possible. One result, whether anticipated or not, was the perception that the company had been victimized along with its customers.[69]

This example of performance at uncertainty demonstrates that there are two ways to approach a catastrophe such as a large security breach. First, the organization can take a risk management approach, focusing on closing the tap of loss and preventing further problems. This approach ignores the losses to customers while focusing on mitigating the effect on the organization. Second is an aggressive program meant to exploit the situation to keep customer loyalty intact and even to improve it, to "clean house" in some ways, even if largely symbolic (such as replacing the CEO), and by navigating the uncertainty of how customers and markets react by taking the most positive approach possible to improve relations on all levels.

The decision to go with the second program is a judgment call. But more than anything else, the decision is a reflection of the organizational culture. On a longer-term basis, this strategy creates *more* growth rather than impedes it. Is this one variety of how growth trumps risk? Yes! By turning the cyberattack into a series of positive action steps, the company was able to focus on strategy risk and move forward. It is the essence of performance at uncertainty.

As a cyberattack is beyond the immediate control of the growth leader, it is also crucial to recognize that uncertainty and risk are vastly different. A brief analysis of these two ideas is worth considering.

---

[69] Anat Hovac and Paul Gray, "The Ripple Effect of an Information Security Breach: A Stakeholder Analysis," *Communications of the Association for Information Systems*, vol. 34, article 50, February 2014.

Walking the Tightrope

Uncertainty and risk are entirely different. Risk encompasses a series of possible occurrences that can be imagined and contemplated, whose recovery strategies can be planned, and whose total cost can be accurately estimated. But nowhere in this process does the discussion involve the concept of advantage. Uncertainty is more intriguing because it encompasses the universe of the unknown and points out how priorities can be set with markets in mind.

How do you create growth while retaining value? This priority appears during periods of strong improvement in markets but can become a negative if not controlled.

Growth, to many, simply means higher revenue and profits every year. However, a more enlightened view of growth is that it has to be permanent. Growth is not a reference to profits but to moving the organization forward. This is the priority.

When I say that growth trumps risk, that is what I mean. In the profit-based mind-set with focus on FUD, compliance, and performance, emphasis is invariably placed on risk questions. What is the risk of an initiative? What does it cost? What are the alternatives? In this mind-set, market advantage itself is so risky that it may be worth avoiding. This is a big problem. A case of a disastrous set of decisions, entered into by Volkswagen, makes this point. In some cases, growth doesn't just trump risk, it tramples it.

The Great Volkswagen Debacle

The well-known VW brand was tarnished in 2015 when it was disclosed the company had redesigned turbocharged direct injection (TDI) software in their diesel engine models to report passing emissions tests artificially. As a result, levels of nitrogen oxide (NO_x) passed tests but actually were producing up to forty times higher. This affected an estimated 11 million cars worldwide for cars built between 2009 and 2015.[70]

---

[70] Jack Ewing, "Volkswagen Says 11 Million Cars Worldwide Are Affected in Diesel Deception," *The New York Times*, September 22, 2015.

On September 18, 2015, the EPS served VW with a notice of violation, charging "defective device" firmware was installed. Initially, Volkswagen said discrepancies were technical glitches and nothing more. After being confronted with evidence, however, the company admitted to manipulation of tests. Martin Winterkorn, CEO, said,

> I am shocked by the events of the past few days. I am stunned that misconduct on such a scale was possible in the Volkswagen Group. As CEO I accept responsibility for the irregularities. I am doing this in the interests of the company even though I am not aware of any wrongdoing on my part.[71]

Volkswagen further admitted that 11 million cars were affected and placed aside more than $7 billion to fix the software. Another 1.2 million in the United Kingdom were also affected.[72]

The important lesson here is that shortcuts undertaken with financial motives cost much more in profits and reputation than any savings once the deception becomes known. All stakeholders suffer, and consequently, growth does *not* occur. Not only is the intended savings unrealized, the actual loss to all stakeholders is disastrous. The stock price alone reveals the impact on investors of this scandal.

The consequences here say much about growth. When markets are hot and profits are good, the temptation is there to pursue financial gains. It's unwise, however, to ignore the financial risk, not to mention in this case the ethical risk in this pursuit.

Other companies have learned a different lesson. They have learned that growth trumps risk in every sense. Even if the issue is looked at only with a financial lens, the true risks involved are not worth the expense of growth. Once the cheat is revealed, it will cost much more to remedy the problem through corrective action, fines, and lawsuits

---

[71] Martin Winterkorn, resignation statement, September 23, 2015.
[72] "1.2m UK vehicles affected in VW scandal," *BBC News*, September 30, 2015.

than any possible savings could ever justify. The previous case histories reveal an equally deadly error compared to a wise management of strategy risk. Once again, the contrast here is between how two companies dealt with growth and the potential of growth. One pursued quality, and the other chased profits.

Illustration 17: Volkswagen stock chart

The overriding lesson of these case histories is clear; growth trumps risk *because* it is market driven. It has to be a priority because it is the only way to deal with the unexpected, the uncertainty of life. Johnson & Johnson and TJX were able to confront a huge problem and create market advantage by operating on the basic principle that growth is the priority, not by reducing exposure or cutting costs. GM and VW made mistakes in different ways, but the common element was their failure to recognize how to create permanent growth.

The whole idea of growth requires abandoning the outmoded points of view about risk. Although risk management is essential as an operating process, it is not oriented toward markets and growth creation. Because growth trumps risk, growth leaders have to focus on what works long term while bringing along traditional risk managers as part of the team to create value. This is a very large challenge, but by focusing on competencies, capabilities, and mind-sets, growth leaders will be able to make their case and convert others to the uncertainty advantage.

Nothing speaks to a mind-set like success.

Epilogue
The Circle of Uncertainty

The uncertainty advantage is inspired by the five overriding principles of focus, navigation, urgency, details, and priority. These five principles are unleashed by relevant capabilities, nimble competencies, and an objective mind-set. When leaders, managers, and the market work together, these principles are transformative. However, none are priorities. All have equal importance and impact as elements of the uncertainty advantage. The final step is to act personally to put the new thinking in place.

The uncertainty advantage principles have been described through the previous five chapters (focus, navigation, priority, urgency, and relentless pursuit of cause and effect). These are not sequential; they are of equal value and importance and represent segments of the whole. They also provide guideposts for execution.

Many have published papers and books that touch on these concepts, and these have been referred to throughout the book. However, none of these published sources have articulated the whole idea. Focus remains on risk management. Even when uncertainty is mentioned, it is still expressed as something to manage. By its nature, uncertainty cannot be managed. It must be navigated.

The UTA and five principles form the initial strategy for achieving the market advantage. Faced with a situation (change, expectations, decision[s], and uncertainty), the leader enlists the competencies and capabilities of managers to pursue the uncertainty advantage.

There is no doubt that these principles provide the framework for a form of new thinking about strategy. Leaders may recognize the limitations of existing risk strategies by understanding how this all works. It does not mean risk management has to be abandoned. It is a valuable operational process, providing essential services to the organization. It is reactive. It should be viewed and applied in context, however. It is *not* part of a process aimed at creating market advantage. For that, you need to embrace and exploit uncertainty.

Setting up a Value Chain

Uncertainty creates the links in the value chain itself. As traditionally understood, this value chain is based on risk analysis.

> In designing their value chains, companies typically focus on three things: revenue ... cost structure ... and resource velocity ... In thinking through changes to the business model, therefore, it is essential to examine the major sources of risk ...[73]

The authors next observe that this effort, "can also reveal unsuspected opportunities for creating value by adding risk – if the company is well-placed to manage it."[74] This, essentially, is the uncertainty advantage. This is exactly how companies reduce uncertainty on the demand side by navigating it to create market advantage, not through risk management initiatives, but by better understanding the benefits that uncertainty provides.

This approach recognizes that a reactive look at risk is ineffective, and when properly viewed, risk drives innovation. The uncertainty

---

[73] Karen Girotra and Serguei Netessine, "How to Build Risk into Your Business Model," *Harvard Business Review,* May 2011.
[74] Ibid.

inherent in all risk can be navigated in a proactive manner; once again referring to the five principles in the circle of uncertainty.

If uncertainty is embraced as part of the new thinking, it is essential to also acknowledge that the traditional approach to risk and risk management cannot be used to set up market advantage. It's that simple. This observation was well expressed in a speech delivered in 2014.

> We are under attack by change. The marketplace and battle-space are increasingly populated by peer competitors and those who can achieve competitive advantage with limited resources. The value of traditional approaches is eroding. We can no longer gain and maintain our strategic position in an industry, market or contested area the way we used to. Cheap and abundant supply chains, the internet, easy user interfaces and the free flow of interpersonal connections over social media challenge our traditional models.[75]

All of these factors contribute to what I have observed in this book. In the chaos of the unexpected—events that dominate organizational activity and behavior—a focus on risk management will not accomplish your desired outcomes. It is not enough to react.

Uncertainty and the process of using it begins with a change/trigger, leading to action based on an expected outcome. The underlying assumptions going into this flow (risk management versus uncertainty navigation) determine the actual outcome. This also explains why a majority of processes based on traditional assumptions fail. Uncertainty relies on your cultural degree of belief in how well events can be controlled (navigated) and led to a successful conclusion (market advantage).

Because a majority of managers have no faith in the ability to convert uncertainty into market advantage, failure often is predetermined.

---

[75] Mark Phillips, "Uncertainty as Competitive Advantage," Speech, Hong Kong Theater, December 1, 2014, http://www.lse.ac.uk.

However, applying data, talent, tools, and processes to the question of navigation—as the many cases histories in preceding chapters have proven—does overcome the pessimism that permeates organizational thinking. Behavioral inhibitors are the most difficult aspect of this. Suppression, bias, neglect, ignorance, noise, incompetence, and lack of clarity all make your task especially challenging. Even if you subscribe to the new thinking of the uncertainty advantage, how do you overcome these blocking attributes of an organization's culture?

The process is challenging even though the answer is simple. A growth leader not only takes initiative but is also able to convert the negative behaviors and gain true believers. The Jack Welch experience at GE might appear simple in hindsight, but he had to not only set up a six sigma process to change internal actions but also convert an entire culture and begin a dialogue leading to change. That culture was deeply embedded over many decades. Only through strong growth leadership was Welch able to accomplish the big change in GE. His technique was described as

> Jack Welch used the mantra of "speed, simplicity, and self-confidence" as the beacon for his transformation of GE's culture in the 1990's — in stark contrast to the company's analytical, bureaucratic, and hierarchical culture at the time. This aspirational vision sparked dialogue at every level of the company about what people needed to do to make GE successful — and to be personally successful at GE.[76]

Forgetting for the moment the "nice guy" image of Welch, the reality is that growth leaders have to be tough and even ruthless. Changing a culture is not a suggestion but a requirement, and a growth leader has to demand that people go along with the ideas that work or else.

---

[76] Ron Ashkenas, "You Can't Dictate Culture—but You Can Influence It," *Harvard Business Review*, June 21, 2011.

The real turning point for GE's transformation came when Jack Welch publicly announced to his senior managers that he had fired two business leaders for not demonstrating the new behaviors of the company — despite having achieved exceptional financial results. This made it very clear that the culture was not just a soft concept — instead, it had tangible outcomes and consequences.[77]

Uncertainty as a Negative

We all tend to dislike uncertainty. It brings into question all of our assumptions and introduces previously unconsidered exposures. As long as uncertainty is treated as a negative, no growth will be possible. Nothing grows in times of certainty. Nothing changes, and nothing is questioned. Uncertainty is the great catalyst for progress. This is an unavoidable truth.

Even with our dislike of uncertainty within the organization, we tend to like it when applied to mysteries, games, puzzles, and even gambling. By beating the odds, we like to believe we can overcome uncertainty. In truth, however, those who win apply one of two techniques. Bluffing (at a poker table, for example) introduces great uncertainty. The other players have to try and read you. Do you have a good hand, or are you bluffing? Uncertainty.

The second technique is more difficult to spot. It is the management of uncertainty through calculated analysis of a situation. If you are playing poker, you observe the "tell" of other players, or you calculate the percentages of likelihood that your hand will win or lose. This ability appears repetitively among growth leaders who have overcome the negative view of uncertainty and have learned to see it as an opportunity.

These growth leaders might not express their approaches in

---

[77] Ibid.

quantified terms, but they do apply a sort of uncertainty advantage index. This is a measurement of odds for success or failure, a method for analyzing a situational risk with all known factors in play. This index asks what we are uncertain about and whether our actions can influence the expected outcome.

The index further turns the negative into a positive by asking how well the organization objectively understands and addresses its own vulnerabilities. In risk management, this is a given, and the task is one of mitigation and transfer. In the uncertainty advantage, the issues are viewed from the marketing lens instead of the operational, financial, and compliance lenses.

To overcome the negative attitude within your organization's culture, you need to determine how to convert uncertainty in a marketing sense and within a competitive landscape. How do you create growth out of the uncertainty itself? This is where the five principles are applied for maximum effectiveness. Simply stating this as a theory is only the beginning. However, looking back at the case histories, you see it again and again; growth leaders have been able to create market advantage by drastically changing attitudes about uncertainty and by converting the internal culture.

This is not an easy task, but it is essential. It requires the connection of strategy through execution. Easy to say, but more difficult to do. Uncertainty is not only an organizational matter but a deeply personal one as well. We all face uncertainty in every aspect of our lives, even down to the mundane. Will it rain tomorrow? If I take my normal route to work, will I be in an accident? If I take a different course, will I be in an accident? Should I stay in bed today? What if a plane crashes into my house and kills me? In every moment of life, uncertainty is present. By avoiding uncertainty, as many organizations try to do through risk management initiatives, we only deceive ourselves to believe we have some control. It makes more sense to accept and embrace uncertainty as opportunity. That is the basic message of this book.

No one expects change to occur overnight or without the requisite struggle that it involves. However, recognizing the proper place for risk management as an operational process is the first step in moving outside of the operational box and beginning to embrace the new thinking in an effective and dynamic way. What I call the uncertainty advantage is simply an effective concept for creating market advantage, something not possible with any operational process (like risk management).

My odyssey from a career as risk manager to this new insight has not been quick, and it has not been of my own doing. I have come to a set of realizations, not through any genius of my own, but by working with and observing the inspirational growth leaders in many industries and seeing a consistent set of attributes. I was fortunate to find myself in a position to work with many growth leaders over the years, and this is the perch from which I was able to identify the common attributes—focus on permanent growth and not on profits, ability to think outside of the risk box, the guts to suggest market-driven initiatives, and more than anything else, a talent for understanding uncertainty as a positive force for change.

About the Author

Gary Lynch earned a bachelor of science degree in finance from the New York Institute of Technology. He is the author of two previous books, *At Your Own Risk* (John Wiley, 2008) and *Single Point of Failure* (John Wiley, 2009). This book represents an evolution in his thoughts about the core business challenges of our times, and how risk management is maturing and becoming a more market-driven process of uncertainty navigation.

Lynch is founder and CEO of The Risk Project, LLC, an advisory and research firm. He was formerly a managing director and the global leader of Marsh's Risk Intelligence and Resiliency Strategies practice, a partner at Booz Allen Hamilton and Ernst & Young, research director at the Gartner Group, and chief information security officer and resiliency officer at Chase Manhattan Bank (now JPMorgan Chase) and Prudential. Under his direction, Marsh earned the distinction of "Top 25 Information Manager" by *Information Management* magazine and "World's Best Supply Chain Risk Consulting Provider" by *Global Finance* magazine. Lynch also served as adviser to the World Economic Forum Global (WEF) Risk Network from 2005 to 2013), and was appointed to the US Department of Commerce's Advisory Committee on Supply Chain Competitiveness. He was also a contributing author to *Supply Chain Disruptions: Theory and Practice of Managing Risk*, chapter 12 (Springer, 2012). Lynch also serves as a Senior Research Fellow for the Supply Chain Management Center at the University of Maryland's Robert H. Smith School of Business.

Lynch has been a panelist and featured speaker for Asia Pacific Economic Cooperation (APEC), World Customs Organization (WCO),

Global Entreopolis@Singapore, National Association of Corporate Directors (NACD), the Risk and Insurance Management Society (RIMS), and Australian Risk Management and Insurance Society (RMIS). He has been a guest lecturer at numerous universities, including NYU's Stern School of Management, MIT's Center for Transportation and Logistics, and Wharton's Center for Risk Management and Decision Processes.

The US Secret Service recognized Lynch with a commendation for September 11, 2001, disaster response and support activity, and he received a Silver Medal of Valor from the Nassau County Fire Service.

Index

A Personal Transformation 51
Academy of Management Executive 123n.
Acceleron Pharma xi, 26, 42n.
Advisory Committee on Supply Chain Competitiveness 6n.
AIG/Lexington 24, 118-120
Alphabet, Inc. 9
Amazon.com xiv, 29, 141
American Trucking Association (ATA) 107
Andretti, Mario 112
An Innovative Growth Leader– Intel 45-49
AONBenfield 104n.
Apple 4, 5, 29, 94, 141
Ashkenas, Ron 162n.
Associated Press 140n.
Association for Financial Professionals 135n.
Association for Information Systems, 153 n.
At Your Own Risk 52, 167
Autodata Corp. 110
Avery, Karen x, 56
Basel III 33
BBC News 122n., 155n.
Bezos, Jeff xiv, 5, 49, 101, 141
Blockbuster 26, 81n., 144, 145

Bloomberg 121n.
Blue Cross/Blue Shield (BCBS) 35-38
Blue Ocean Strategy 64
Branson, Richard 49
Brin, Sergay xiv
Building Resilience in Supply Chains 7
Cantor Fitzgerald 106
Carnegie, Andrew 49
CARS (Car Allowance Rebate System) 88-89
cash for clunkers 91
Caterpillar 107, 108, 112
Centers for Disease Control (CDC) 19n., 22
CFO Innovation 40n.
Champine, Laura 106
Chevrolet Cobalt 109
China Ocean Shipping 106
Chrysler 24, 149-151
Chu, Kathy 104n.
CIBA 137
Circle of Uncertainty 159, 161
Cisco 29, 127
Clothier, Mark 121n.
Commodization of the Starbucks Experience 82
Communications of the Association for Information Systems 153n.
Comparison of Strategies 55-56

Compliance/rules xvi, xix, 33, 38-39, 52, 54, 56, 142-143, 146, 148
component resiliency index (CRI) 131-133
Computerworld 103n.
conditional value at risk (CVaR) 41
Cook, Tim 5, 94
Cottingham, Richard 36
Courtney, Hugh 39n., 115n.
Covey, Stephen xxii
Coyne, John 102
Cummins 107-108, 112
Davis, Carole 121
Deepwater Horizon xvi
Deimler, Mike 127n.
Deloitte 40n.
DeMarie, Samuel M 123n.
Department of Commerce 6, 167
detailed landscape of uncertainty 29-30, 34, 135-137
D'Innocenzio, Anne 140n.
DuPont 120, 121
Ebola breakout 19, 34
Einstein, Albert xv
Elberse, Anita 81
Elite Materials 31
Ellison, Larry 49, 141
Enterprise Risk Management (ERM) 39, 57, 58, 135, 136
Environmental Protection Agency (EPA) 107, 112, 155
Ericcson 115-117
Essilor xvi
European Union (EU) xvi, 8
Evans, Stephen 122n.
Evonik 120, 121-124
Ewing, Jack 154n.
Facebook 26, 141
Fahey, Jonathan 140n.

Failure of Risk Management: Why It's Broken and How to Fix It 15n.
Fairchild Semiconductor 46
Fear, Uncertainty, Doubt (FUD) 32, 33, 34, 35, 54-56, 66, 147-148, 154
F. Hoffmann-La Roche Pharmaceuticals xvi, 20-23, 24, 81, 129
Fisher, Anne 86n.
Fortune 86n.
Freedman, Anne 92n.
Friedman, Thomas L. xv
Fuller, Thomas 102n.
Gates, Bill 82
GE Capital xi, 56, 130-131
General Electric 53
General Motors 24
Girotra, Karen 160n.
Global Risk Network 7
Google xi, xiv, xix
Gordon, Joanne 71n.
Gramm-Leach-Bliley Act 33
Gray, Paul 153n.
great Volkswagen debacle 154-157
Grove, Andy 5, 45-49
growth leader ix, 12, 16, 23, 55, 63, 66, 96, 111, 115, 118, 150, 153, 162
Growth trumps risk 70, 145, 148, 153-156
H1N1/Swine Flu and H5N1/Avian Flu 19
Harvard Business Review 14, 39n., 64n., 98n., 115n., 127n., 160n., 162n.
Hastings, Reed xiv
Henke, John W. Jr. 150n.
Hepper, Doug xi, 79-80
Hit Making, Risk Taking, and the Big Business of Entertainment 81n.
Hitt, Michael A. 123n.

Hong Kong Theater 161n.
Horn, Alan 81
Hovac, Anat 153n.
Hubbard, Doug 15n.
Huntsman xi, 24, 137-139
Huntsman, Peter 138
Hyundai North America xi, 8-9, 10-13, 24, 44, 74-75, 79, 81, 88-90, 91, 93, 107, 111, 114, 122, 129
IHS iSuppli 102
Immelt, Jeffrey 53
Intel 24, 45-48, 58
Irwin, James xi, 21-23
ISX12 engine 108
Iyer, Ramkumay 106n.
Jaffe, Richard 107
Jobs, Steve 5, 29, 49, 101, 141
Johnson & Johnson 148-149, 152, 156
Josephs, Leslie 106n.
JPMorganChase 29, 56, 167
Kaplan, Robert S. 98n.
Kapner, Suzanne 106n.
Keats, Barbara W 123n.
Kessler, Aaron M. 110n.
key performance indicators (KPI's) 54, 130
Kim, W. Chan 64n.
Kirkland, Jane 39n., 115n.
Kotter, John 135
Krafcik, John xi, xix, 9-12, 75, 88-89, 90, 114
Kroc, Ray 49
Lam, J. 135n., 136n.
Landscape varies based on strategies employed 34-40
leader ix, x, xi, xiii, xiv-xxii, 1, 3, 5, 7-14, 15-22, 23-30, 31-34, 40, 43, 45-49, 51-57, 60, 61-70, 71, 73-78, 80-90, 91, 92-93, 97, 99-103, 106, 107, 110-112, 113, 114-115, 118-120, 122, 123, 127, 129-133, 136, 138, 141-143, 145, 146, 147, 148-153, 156-157, 159-165
Leibinger, Peter xi, 76
Maersk Line 106
manager x, xi, xiv, xv, xvii, xviii, xix, xxi, 3, 5, 9, 12-17, 19, 21-22, 27, 30, 31, 33, 35, 39-40, 45, 47-48, 51-52, 54, 56, 57, 60-61, 66-70, 73, 75, 78, 85, 90-91, 96, 99, 100, 103, 111, 114-115, 123, 129-132, 136, 141, 145-148, 156, 159, 161, 163, 165
market differentiator xvii, xix, xxii, 5, 10, 30, 49, 92, 114
Market driven 5, 8, 17-20, 34
market opportunity xiv, xxii, 16, 30, 68, 71, 89, 110, 127
Marshall's 151
Marsh McLennan 56
Mauborgne, Renee 64n.
McCormick 24
Mearian, Lucas 103n.
Mikes, Anette 98n.
Musk, Elon xiv, 5
Nader, François xi, 26, 42
Nan Ya Plastics 31
National Resource Defense Council (NRDC) 108
NBC 81
Netessine, Serguei 160n.
Netflix xiv, 26
New York Times 47n., 102n., 110n., 154n.
Nocera, Andrew 47n.
Nokia 24, 76, 115-116, 129
nongovernment organizations (NGO's) xvi

NPS Pharma xi, 24, 26, 42n.
NVIDIA xvi, 24, 124-127
Occupational Health and Safety Administration (OSHA) 33
Office of Insurance Commission (Thailand) 104
Only the Paranoid Survive 47n.
Onward 71n., 83, 84n.
opportunity ix, x, xiii, xvix, xx, xxii, 1, 3-4, 6, 7-11, 16, 18-23, 24, 25-26, 30-33, 38, 40, 44, 45-49, 52-54, 58-59, 62-65, 67-71, 73-75, 77-78, 79-81, 82, 89, 90, 91, 93, 95-96, 99, 106-107, 109, 110, 113-115, 119-120, 122, 125, 127, 130-131, 134, 138, 139-140, 142, 148, 153, 163, 164
Oracle 141
original equipment manufacturers (OEM's) xvi, 103, 105, 114, 124
Oshika Peninsula 30
Otsuka xi, xvi, 24, 142-145
PA-12 121-122
Page, Larry xiv
PayPal xiv
Pengue, Dan xi, 130
Performance/asset 33, 41, 54
Performance at uncertainty 151-153
Performance-based Strategies 55, 68, 73, 145, 148
Phillips, Mark 161n.
Porter, Michael 14n.
Port of Oakland 106
PriceWaterhouseCoopers x, 56
Rana Plaza 139
Ratner, Gilda 48n.
Reeves, Martin 127n.
Reuters 94, 106n.
Risconomics 24

risk ix-x, xi, xiii, xiv, xv-xviii, xix-xxii, 1, 5, 6-9, 11-15, 19, 21, 23-27, 29-30, 32-35, 38, 39-42, 48-49, 51-59, 61-62, 65, 66, 69, 70, 73, 75-79, 81n., 87, 91-92, 95, 96-101, 104, 105, 107, 108, 110, 111, 116, 118, 119-121, 124, 125-127, 130-138, 139-140, 141-153, 154-156, 159, 160-161, 164-165
Risk and Insurance Magazine 92n.
Roche xi, xvi, 20-23, 24, 81, 129
Rockefeller, John 48
Rockwell Automation xi, xvi, 24, 131-133
Sarbanes Oxley Act (SOX) 33
Schultz, Howard xiv, 49, 71n., 82-88
Self-Driving Car Group xi, xix, 9
Serial killer among us 35-38
Serial Killers: The Method and Madness of Monsters 36n.
Setting up a value chain 160-163
Severe Acute Respiratory Syndrome (SARS) 19
Show Me the Value 23-26
Silverman, Ben 81
Single Point of Failure 23n., 52, 76, 117n.
Solvency II 33
SpaceX xiv
Stallkamp, Thomas T. 150n.
Starbucks xi, xiv, xvi, 24, 29, 71n., 81-88
Stevens, Laura 106n.
Strategy risk tipping point 91-92
supply chain xi, xviii, 4, 5, 6, 7, 19, 23, 52, 76, 97, 100, 101, 106n., 107, 120, 125, 133, 134, 143, 145, 150n., 167
Supply Chain Management Review 150n.

supply chain risk management
(SCRM) 23n., 52n., 76
Tamiflu 21
Tegra® mobile processors 124
Tesla xiv, 141
The World is Flat: A Brief History of the 21st Century xv
TJMax 24
TJX Companies 106-107, 151-153, 156
Today's Trucking 108n.
torso killer 36
Toyota 109-112
transparency xvi
Trudell, Craig 121n.
Trumpf xi, xvi, 24, 66, 76-81
Turning disaster into opportunity 79-81
Tylenol 148-151
Ube Industries 120, 121
Uncertainty as the disrupter 88-91
Unleashing the uncertainty advantage xx, 146-147
Urgent and uncertain industry 124-127
value at Risk (VaR) 41
value chain 130, 145, 160-162
value creator xviii
value enabler xviii, 10, 12
Viguerie, Patrick 39n.
visionary xiii, xiv, 5, 85-86, 115, 119, 120
Vision-Ease Lenses (VEL) 79, 80n., 81, 123
VM Magazine 80n.
Volkswagen 24, 35, 154-155
Vronsky, Peter 36n.
Wall Street Journal 75n., 104n., 106n.
Walton, Sam 49
Wang, Michele 110n.

Warner Brothers 81
Welch, Jack xiv, 49, 162-163
Western Digital 24, 102-105
Whirlpool 24, 91-94
Why is the uncertainty opportunity urgent? 114-115
Winterkorn, Martin 71n., 155
Woo, Grace xi
Workiva 136n.
World Economic Forum 7
World Health Organization (WHO) 22
Xirallic 74, 81, 91, 120
XPI fuel system 108
Yeniyurt, Sengun 150n.
Zhang, Fang 102
Zuckerberg, Mark 26, 141
Zucker, Jeff 81
Zurich 24, 118-120